CHRISTIANITY

Christianity

Michael Keene

LION
ACCESS
GUIDES

Copyright © 2002 Michael Keene
This edition copyright © 2002
Lion Publishing

The author asserts the moral right
to be identified as the author of this work

Published by
Lion Publishing plc
Mayfield House, 256 Banbury Road,
Oxford OX2 7DH, England
ISBN 0 7459 5064 7

First edition 2002
10 9 8 7 6 5 4 3 2 1 0

A catalogue record for this book is
available from the British Library

Typeset in 10.25/11 Venetian 301
Printed and bound in China

Text acknowledgments
Revised English Bible with the Apocrypha
copyright © 1989 by Oxford University
Press and Cambridge University Press.
Scriptures quoted from the Good News
Bible are published by The Bible Societies/
HarperCollins Publishers Ltd, UK ©
American Bible Society 1966, 1971, 1976,
1992, and used with permission.
Scripture quotations taken from the *Holy
Bible, New International Version*, copyright ©
1973, 1978, 1984 by International Bible
Society. Used by permission of Hodder &
Stoughton Limited. All rights reserved.
'NIV' is a registered trademark of
International Bible Society. UK trademark
number 1448790.
Extracts from the Apostles' Creed and the
Nicene Creed, copyright © The Central
Board of Finance of the Church of England.

'Eternal God, the Lord of life' from *The
Methodist Worship Book*, copyright © 1999
Trustees for Methodist Church Purposes.
Used by permission of Methodist
Publishing House.
The Hail Mary, copyright © Catholic
Truth Society.
'Hymn to Matter', from *Hymn of the Universe*
by Pierre Teilhard de Chardin, published by
Georges Borchardt, Inc; *Hymne à la Matière*
by Pierre Teilhard de Chardin, copyright ©
1961 Editions du Seuil.

Picture acknowledgments
Please see page 160.

Contents

Note
Throughout this book the
convention is followed of
dating events by the
abbreviations BCE (Before
Common Era) and CE (Common
Era). They correspond precisely
to the more familiar BC and AD
but avoid giving offence to
those followers of non-
Christian religions who do not
recognize the birth of Christ as
a decisive event in history.

Introducing Christianity

Christianity began in the Roman province of Palestine (present-day Israel, Palestine and Jordan) over 2,000 years ago and is based on the life, teachings, death and resurrection of Jesus Christ. Although Jesus only taught for three years and died an apparently ignominious death on a cross outside Jerusalem, his birth is now celebrated around the world and is the major point from which time is measured, even by non-Christians.

Christianity grew initially as a radical movement within the much older tradition of Judaism. Jesus was a Jew and he remained faithful throughout his life to the Jewish faith, but, after his death, the new religion spread more widely among the Gentiles than the Jews. Christianity soon developed a life of its own, apart from its mother faith, although the link between the two remained complex and problematic for a long time.

As Christianity spread beyond the Roman empire, the life and teachings of

Jesus remained at the heart of the faith. While other religions recognize Jesus as a great teacher and prophet, Christians believe that he is God, or 'the Son of God', who took on human form in order to restore the relationship between God and humankind that had

been broken by human sin and disobedience. They believe that Jesus was crucified and rose again, thus breaking the hold of sin and death, and that today he reigns as Lord of all creation. A Christian can have a personal relationship with God through Christ and can live in the power of the Holy Spirit. Christianity is not,

however, solely concerned with personal salvation; it is also about creating a community of believers (the Church) and responding to the radical teachings of Jesus about social and ethical behaviour.

Today Christianity is the world's largest religion.

It has a wider geographical spread than any other faith with some 1,500 million followers throughout the world. In its early years, Christianity was most securely established in Western countries, largely thanks to the conversion of the Roman emperor Constantine in 312 CE. However, Christianity is now declining numerically in Western countries, although it continues to expand elsewhere. The most rapid growth in the 20th century was in South America and Africa, and this shows every likelihood of continuing into the foreseeable future.

The four Gospels of Matthew, Mark, Luke and John in the New Testament provide the only real historical information we have about Jesus, but they are not straightforward biographies in the modern sense. They were written by committed followers of Jesus who used their information to make a spiritual statement about the beginning of God's kingdom with the coming of Jesus, the Son of God and the Saviour of human-kind.

The Gospels tell us that, after being baptized by John the Baptist in the River Jordan at the age of 30, Jesus began a public ministry that lasted for just three years. One of his first acts was to choose 12 disciples who stayed with him, almost intact, until the end. Jesus spent much time teaching them

The Crucifixion (fresco) by the School of Giotto.

and preparing them to continue his work after he left the earth. He also preached to a much wider audience. Alongside this teaching, the Gospels record a number of miracles performed by Jesus – such as the feeding of the 5,000 and the raising of Lazarus from the dead.

Before long, however, Jesus' religious enemies were scheming to bring about his death. Eventually Pontius Pilate, the Roman procurator of Judea, ordered Jesus' execution. His death took place on a hill called Calvary or Golgotha outside the city of Jerusalem, probably in 29 CE. Three days later, God brought Jesus back to life – the resurrection. Jesus' death and resurrection stand at the very heart of the Christian faith because they are the means by which God has secured the salvation of humankind.

Forty days later the Holy Spirit was given to the early Christians on the Day of Pentecost and the Christian Church was born.

> *For us men and for our salvation he came down from heaven; by the power of the Holy Spirit he became incarnate of the Virgin Mary and was made man. For our sake he was crucified under Pontius Pilate; he suffered death and was buried. On the third day he rose again.*
>
> NICENE CREED

JESUS AND THE EARLY CHURCH

Contents

The Story Begins

Apart from one or two brief, and inconclusive, references to Jesus by Jewish and Roman historians, our entire knowledge of him comes from the four Gospels in the New Testament.

By the time that Jesus was born the Romans had ruled Palestine with an iron fist for decades. For most of their history the Jewish people had yearned for the coming of the Messiah, a figure long promised by God, who would deliver them from their enemies and inaugurate a kingdom of peace and prosperity for Israel. There were many ideas swirling around at the time about the Messiah but most Jews hoped that he

I consider you to be the servant of God and I love you more, the more you are attacked by temptations. Truly I tell you: no one should consider himself a perfect friend of God until he has passed through many temptations and tribulations.

ST FRANCIS OF ASSISI (1182–1226),
ITALIAN FOUNDER OF
THE FRANCISCAN ORDER

would be a warrior – one strong enough to lead them in a victorious uprising against their Roman overlords. Some Jews lost patience, could not

THE NAME OF JESUS

Jesus Christ was not the proper name of Jesus. Jesus, or Joshua, means 'God is Saviour'. Christ was a title and derives from the Greek word for 'Messiah' – the one chosen by God for a special and unique mission. Jesus' real name was probably something like Jesus bar Joseph, meaning 'Jesus son of Joseph'.

wait any longer for God and joined a group of freedom fighters plotting the violent overthrow of the Romans – the Zealots. Others known as the Essenes took a more sanguine and less extreme view, withdrawing into the desert to pray, study and wait for the coming of the Messiah.

The birth of Jesus

Jesus, then, was born into a highly volatile country. His actual birth took place in Bethlehem, Judea, around 4 BCE. Because the town was overcrowded with visitors for the Roman census, Jesus was born in a stable, a scene re-enacted in nativity plays across the world each Christmas. Yet the Gospel writers make clear that Jesus' birth was far from ordinary. They describe how angels proclaimed him the promised Saviour and they present his conception as a miraculous one, his mother Mary being a virgin.

Jesus was born in Judea, a small corner of the Roman empire. At the time of Jesus the Romans controlled all of the Western Mediterranean.

The Gospels, therefore, portray Jesus as both fully human and fully divine.

One Gospel writer records how Herod the Great, the ruler of Judea, tried to kill the infant Jesus by ordering the massacre of all boys under the age of two in the area. This forced Mary and Joseph, Jesus' parents, to hurriedly take him to Egypt. On Herod's death the family returned to Nazareth where Jesus grew up, probably worked in his father's carpentry shop and finally emerged into public prominence at the age of 30.

Jesus' Jewish upbringing meant that he would have been circumcised when he was eight days old and paid weekly visits to worship in the local synagogue on the Sabbath day. Occasionally he would have been taken to the Temple in Jerusalem for special festivals such as the Passover. On one such occasion Jesus stayed behind to quiz the Jewish religious leaders on their faith after his parents had left for home. This is the only incident recorded in the Gospels between Jesus' infancy and his emergence from obscurity to become a highly controversial public figure, so was clearly considered to be significant.

Baptism and Temptations

Jesus asked John the Baptist to baptize him and afterwards both God the Father and the Holy Spirit set their seal on his coming ministry. Jesus' commitment was to be fully tested by his temptations in the desert.

Although many 'holy men' in Palestine were offering baptism, John the Baptist was different from them: his baptism was 'for the remission of sins' and had an apocalyptic element, anticipating the end of the world. The people were told that they could only escape the imminent time of judgment by repenting and seeking God's forgiveness.

This is my Son, whom I love; with him I am well pleased.

MATTHEW 3:17

The baptism of Jesus

John was quite adamant. He was not the promised Messiah, as many thought he might be, but he had come to prepare the way for that figure. When Jesus appeared on the banks of the River Jordan requesting baptism, John was both surprised and reluctant. Jesus, though, insisted that it was the right thing for him to do.

When Jesus came up out of the water he saw the heavens above him opened and the Holy Spirit descending on him in a the form of a dove. He also heard the voice of God proclaiming that Jesus was his only Son. This may have been a private revelation to Jesus to set the tone for his ministry ahead – an assurance that he was divine and set apart as God's Messiah.

The temptations

In between Jesus' baptism and the start of his public ministry the Gospel writers agree that he was tempted by the Devil, Satan. This confrontation between the powers of good and evil took place after Jesus had been

John had to be persuaded before he would baptize Jesus. For Jesus, however, it was necessary before his public ministry could begin.

No one is absolutely sure where the practice of baptism originated. We do know, however, that Jewish communities used it to initiate new converts into the faith long before John the Baptist called people to be baptized on the banks of the River Jordan.

The Judean Desert, where Jesus spent 40 days before beginning his ministry. After the 40 days he was tempted by Satan.

physically weakened by a period of 40 days spent fasting. It mirrors the conflict which was to occur frequently throughout his ministry, before reaching its climax in his death on the cross. That death was seemingly the greatest hour for the powers of darkness.

◆ In the first temptation Satan tried to persuade Jesus to use his divine power to satisfy his physical hunger. Jesus responded by saying that it is only the word of God in the scriptures that can truly satisfy human need.

◆ In the second temptation Satan attempted to goad Jesus into throwing himself off the pinnacle of the Temple, since God's angels would surely protect him, but Jesus resisted.

◆ Finally Satan offered Jesus all the kingdoms of the world on the condition that he give up his unique mission and worship the Prince of Darkness.

Jesus was different from other 'messiahs' because he refused to use his power for self-preservation or world domination. At the very beginning he set his stall out for all to see: he could only accomplish God's purpose through rejection, suffering, death and resurrection.

The Disciples

A central feature of the Gospels is Jesus' choice and training of 12 disciples. They exemplified the highs and lows of Christian discipleship as they grappled to understand Jesus and the nature of his kingdom.

For three years after his baptism Jesus taught, preached, healed and ministered throughout Palestine (between about 27 and 30 CE). Early on, Jesus gathered a small group of disciples around himself – the 12 apostles – although a much larger group, including many women, formed an outer circle of followers.

If we are willing to learn the meaning of real discipleship and actually to become disciples, the Church in the West would be transformed, and the resultant impact on society would be staggering.

DAVID WATSON,
ENGLISH ANGLICAN EVANGELIST

The disciples and Jesus

The nation of Israel was built upon 12 tribes in its earliest days and Jesus' choice of the same number of disciples was no coincidence. The new Christian community was to be the 'new' Israel. Jesus promised that at the end of time the disciples would sit on 12 thrones to judge the 12 tribes of Israel. The Gospel accounts vary but each gives details of how some of the individual disciples were called. Two pairs of fishermen – Simon Peter and his brother Andrew plus the brothers James and John – became disciples after Jesus called them on the banks of the Sea of Galilee. Matthew, sometimes called Levi, was collecting taxes for the much-hated Romans when Jesus called him. John, in his Gospel, records the distinctive ways in which Philip and his brother Nathaniel responded to Jesus. Most of the other disciples remain largely unknown although we do know that one of them, another Simon, was a Zealot. Two of the remainder, Judas Iscariot and Thomas, were to play prominent roles in the story of Jesus both before and after the crucifixion.

Discipleship

From time to time Jesus spelled out to his 12 apostles and

other followers the true cost of discipleship. The life of a disciple was to be, above everything else, one of service to others. Jesus made this very clear when, towards the end of his life, he took a bowl of water and washed his apostles' feet – disciple that only those prepared to sacrifice everything could enter God's kingdom.

Almost to the end the disciples failed to grasp that Jesus was going to meet a premature death – despite being given many clear warnings. *Sinodus*, or *Council of the Apostles*, from *The Octateuch: Scenes from the Life of Christ and the Apostles*, Ethiopia, 1744.

an act of great humility. Discipleship is a call to follow the example of Jesus, the Son of man, who sacrificed his life so that many could be saved. Jesus called people to live a life of childlike faith and innocent trust. He told a rich young man who wanted to become a

The Kingdom of God

One theme dominated Jesus' teaching – that of the kingdom of God. When he explained to people how they could enter this kingdom he turned many of the accepted values of his time upside down.

Matthew tells us that what set Jesus apart from the teachers of the Law was that Jesus taught the people 'with authority'. In the Gospels of Matthew, Mark and Luke the central theme of Jesus' teaching is the kingdom of God.

Jesus and God's kingdom

In all four Gospels the early ministry of Jesus was linked with that of John the Baptist, since both of them told the people that the kingdom, or reign, of God was 'close at hand'. However, Jesus went further than John by

As Jesus taught his disciples when he washed their feet, the service of others lies at the heart of God's kingdom. *Christ Washing the Disciples' Feet* (c. 1390) by the Italian School, Arezzo.

announcing that the kingdom had actually arrived with his own coming. The 'good news' of this kingdom was the love and peace which Jesus offered to men and women from all walks of life.

Jesus' teaching about the kingdom of God had two strands:

◆ The kingdom is a moral and spiritual reality in the world today. The rabbis of the time taught that a person became a member of God's kingdom by reciting, and believing, the *Shema*, Israel's confession of faith in the one God. However, Jesus taught people to prepare themselves here and now for the time when God's kingdom would be fully realized on earth. This demands repentance, a wholesale change of heart, through which an individual can accept the arrival of the kingdom as the gospel, God's good news for humanity.

◆ The kingdom looks forward to the time when God will extend his divine rule over everything in creation and vindicate the righteous. People heard this urgent tone in Jesus' voice when he began his public ministry: 'The time has come. The kingdom of God is near. Repent and believe the good news!'

BELONGING TO GOD'S KINGDOM

Membership of God's kingdom was extended to all on exactly the same terms. The religious leaders were invited into the kingdom and some responded. So were the Roman soldiers, the tax collectors, the prostitutes, the Samaritans and the poor. The Beatitudes, presented in Matthew's Gospel as part of Jesus' Sermon on the Mount, describe the spiritual characteristics of those who belong to God's kingdom: 'Blessed are the meek, for they will inherit the earth.'

Around 50 of Jesus' sayings and parables are concerned with the kingdom of God. Matthew uses the phrase 'kingdom of heaven' instead – but there is no difference between this devout Jewish phrase and the 'kingdom of God'.

Miracles

There are many miracles recorded in the Gospels. These acted as a clear sign that the power of God was at work in Jesus. Some branches of the Church continue the healing ministry of Jesus today.

The four Gospels and the Acts of the Apostles in the New Testament record numerous examples of Jesus, and later his apostles, performing miracles. From a biblical point of view a miracle is an instance when God acts in a remarkable way to achieve an extraordinary end. In the New Testament three words are used for 'miracle':

◆ 'Wonder' – an event out of the ordinary which causes a feeling of awe in onlookers, who realize they have been in the presence of God.
◆ 'Sign' – clear evidence that God is at work on earth.
◆ 'Power' – a demonstration of divine might and authority.

Miracles seemed abundant in the Old Testament period, with phenomenal plagues, the parting of the waters of the Reed Sea and the fantastic provision of food for the Israelites in the wilderness. Jesus' miracles reassured the people that God was working supernaturally through him, just as he had worked miraculously in days gone by.

Miraculous signs

Jesus' miracles were intended as a public announcement that he was the expected Messiah, come to usher in God's kingdom. When John the Baptist's disciples asked Jesus whether he was the promised Messiah or not, Jesus pointed to his miraculous activities as the answer.

HEALING AND TODAY'S CHURCH

All the major Churches teach that people should pray for 'wholeness' of body, mind and spirit – for themselves and for others – since this is God's will for everyone. Some Pentecostal and charismatic Churches hold special healing services, in which people lay hands on the sick while offering prayers for their healing. Such Churches view healing as a gift of the Holy Spirit.

Around the time of Jesus there were many so-called 'miracle-workers'. One such was Rabbi Hanina ben Dosa who, towards the end of the first century CE, is said to have healed the son of another rabbi. The description of this in the Talmud bears a very strong resemblance to the story told in John's Gospel, where Jesus heals an official's son.

◆ 'Healing miracles' – such as curing a blind man or healing a deaf and dumb man.

◆ 'Resurrection miracles' – such as restoring Lazarus and a widow's son to life.

Allied to these is the greatest miracle of all in the New Testament – God's raising of Jesus from the dead.

These miracles seldom took place without a display of faith – either by the person concerned or by someone else on their behalf. For example, when some men brought a paralytic to Jesus to be healed, it was their faith which Jesus saw and respected.

The raising of Jairus' daughter. Jesus always carried out miracles for a reason – unlike the majority of other 'miracle-workers' at the time.

The many miracles attributed to Jesus in the New Testament fall into three categories:

◆ 'Nature miracles' – such as walking on the water or calming a storm.

The Last Days

After sharing a last meal with his disciples, Jesus prayed alone in the Garden of Gethsemane before being arrested. Three trials followed – one before High Priest Caiaphas, another before the Jewish Sanhedrin and the last before Pontius Pilate, the Roman governor.

The words and actions of Jesus had a disturbing effect on the religious leaders of the time – especially the Pharisees and the Sadducees. They were particularly upset by Jesus' claim to be their Messiah and they hatched a plot for his arrest and trial.

Jesus answered, 'You are right in saying I am a king. In fact, for this reason I was born, and for this I came into the world, to testify to the truth. Everyone on the side of truth listens to me.' 'What is truth?' Pilate asked.

JOHN 18:37–38

The last night

On the first night of the Passover festival Jesus shared a final meal with his disciples – the Last Supper – and offered them bread and wine to symbolize his forthcoming death. By so doing Jesus bequeathed to the Church two lasting symbols by which it could remember, and celebrate, his death in centuries to come.

After the meal, they all went to the Garden of Gethsemane. Jesus took Peter, James and John ahead with him. In the garden, Jesus prayed that God might deliver him from his imminent suffering, but also that God's will would be done. As he finished praying Judas Iscariot, one of his disciples, arrived with a group of Temple soldiers, who proceeded to arrest him. The remainder of his disciples including Peter, who had just pledged to die rather than desert him, fled and left him friendless. Jesus was on his own.

Jesus on trial

The Gospel accounts of subsequent events vary. After his arrest Jesus was taken to the house of Caiaphas, the High Priest. When Jesus refused to deny that he was the Son of God he was accused of blasphemy – a capital crime in the Jewish community. From there Jesus was taken to appear before the Sanhedrin, the supreme Jewish

The scene in the Garden of Gethsemane when Judas leads the temple guards to arrest Jesus. *The Betrayal of Christ* by Ugolino di Nerio (active 1317, died c. 1339/49).

PONTIUS PILATE

Pontius Pilate was the Roman prefect of Judea from 26 CE to 37 CE. Contemporary opinion suggests that he was a brutal and sadistic ruler who upset the Jews on many occasions. Once he raided the Temple treasury and then, when the people objected, sent in his troops, resulting in a terrible bloodbath. There is some indication that Pilate and his wife later became Christians, however, and the Coptic Orthodox Church honours them as saints and martyrs.

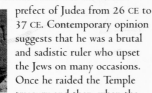

A limestone slab found at Caesarea. The inscription is the only known contemporary one to mention Pontius Pilate.

Council in Jerusalem, but this did not have the power to impose the death sentence without the approval of the Roman governor for the province, Pontius Pilate. According to the Gospels this was a decision that Pilate was reluctant to take but the crowd, stirred into a frenzy by the religious leaders, told him that he would be no friend of Caesar if he freed Jesus. Pilate condemned Jesus to death but only after he had washed his hands to remove the guilt of what was about to happen.

The Death of Jesus

The death of Jesus on the cross is the most important single event to the Christian faith. On the surface it seemed to mark failure at the end of a life that promised so much but, to Christians, it signifies the final defeat of the powers of darkness.

Before his execution Jesus was beaten by the Roman soldiers, just like any other condemned man of the time. After they had scourged him the soldiers flattened a crown of thorns onto his head, placed a reed sceptre in his hand and hailed him in jest as 'king of the Jews'. He was then taken to Golgotha, the Place of the Skull, for execution.

The crucifixion

The four Gospels paint a vivid picture of Jesus' last hours. Having needed the help of bystander Simon of Cyrene to carry part of his cross to Golgotha, Jesus was exhausted even before he was nailed to the cross. He was crucified between two convicted thieves. The Romans always crucified their victims in a public place as a deterrent to others, since

Jesus was put to death between two thieves. One of them recognized Jesus as a king who was entering his kingdom, and sought acceptance from him. Despite his suffering on the cross, Jesus responded to the man's pleas. *The Crucifixion* by Tintoretto (1518–94).

they ruled by fear. Around Jesus' feet a handful of followers knelt and prayed, while the soldiers gambled for the few garments he possessed – their perk for carrying out a thankless task.

The Gospels record the last seven utterances of Jesus from the cross: he asked God to forgive those who caused him to suffer; he encouraged one of the thieves dying beside him; he asked one of his disciples, John, to look after his mother; he cried aloud to God; he expressed despair at his own suffering; he declared that his own mission on earth was over; and he finally committed himself to God's safe keeping.

The Ascension from an 11th-century Italian manuscript, *Meditation on the Life of Christ*.

> *All authority in heaven and on earth has been given to me. Therefore go and make disciples of all nations, baptizing them in the name of the Father and of the Son and of the Holy Spirit, and teaching them to obey everything I have commanded you. And surely I will be with you always, to the very end of the age.*
>
> MATTHEW 28:18–20

The resurrection

According to the Gospel evidence there were hundreds of witnesses to the resurrection of Jesus. After three days in the tomb Jesus appeared to, among others, Mary Magdalene, Peter, two unknown disciples out walking, over 500 people on a mountain in Galilee and the 11 remaining disciples. These appearances occurred during the 40 days prior to his ascension into heaven.

The exact nature of Jesus' 'resurrection body' is a matter of conjecture, although something fundamental had clearly changed: his face was transformed and he was able to suddenly appear and disappear. The disciples and the other followers also changed as a result of their encounter with the risen Jesus.

Just before he ascended into heaven, Jesus commissioned his disciples to continue his work on earth by spreading the gospel message throughout the Roman empire and beyond. He promised them his Holy Spirit to empower them for this task.

The Day of Pentecost

The Christian Church began its long history on the Day of Pentecost, when the disciples received the gift of the Holy Spirit just as Jesus had promised them.

The Acts of the Apostles (by Gospel-writer Luke) describes what happened to Jesus' disciples on the Day of Pentecost. The disciples were gathered together when what sounded like a great wind came down from the sky and what looked like tongues of fire touched each person. The disciples 'were filled with the Holy Spirit and began to speak in other tongues, as the Spirit enabled them'. Three thousand people were baptized that day and the Christian Church was born. The Holy Spirit, who in the Old Testament had only indwelt a few special people such as Moses and David, was now being poured out on all believers.

The message spreads

To begin with, the leader of the new Christian community was Peter but, as an orthodox Jew, he seemed unable to accept the truth that both Jews and Gentiles were equally welcome to enter God's kingdom. Peter was succeeded by Paul, a former persecutor of the Christians, who became a tireless writer and missionary in the work of spreading the Christian gospel. Paul made three exhausting and lengthy missionary journeys and wrote many letters, some of which are included in the New Testament, before losing

THE CHURCH GROWS

During the early years of the Church, Christians continued to worship in their local synagogue or in each other's homes and it was to be many years before special places of worship, churches, were built. There were spasmodic periods of persecution when the Christians were defenceless against the whims of individual Roman emperors, but the Church survived and was strengthened by this testing of its faith. To cope with the increasing number of converts to Christianity the Church began to develop a more elaborate organization. Bishops were appointed to look after the new Christian communities that were forming.

For over 1,000 years the Church, born on the Day of Pentecost, was one although not always united. The first major split in the Church's unity came in 1054 but many others were to follow. At the latest count there are over 22,000 different Christian Churches or denominations.

On the Day of Pentecost, Jesus' disciples were meeting together when the Holy Spirit suddenly came upon them and tongues of fire rested on each person. *Pentecost* by Giotto di Bondone (c. 1267–1337).

Think! We who are mere nonentities can have the same Spirit resting on us as rested upon Moses the friend of God, upon David the beloved king, and upon Elijah the mighty prophet.

WATCHMAN NEE (NEE TO-SHENG), CHINESE EVANGELIST

his life at the hands of Nero, the Roman emperor, around 67 CE. Peter also lost his life around the same time.

Peter

During the ministry of Jesus and in the earliest days of the Christian Church Peter towered over the other apostles and Church leaders. He found it difficult to accept, however, that Jews and non-Jews could enter the Church on an equal footing.

Our information about Peter comes mainly from the four Gospels, the Acts of the Apostles and two letters in the New Testament which are attributed to him. A fisherman by trade, Jesus named him Cephas, Greek for Peter, meaning 'the rock', and he was clearly destined for leadership among the small group of disciples. The Gospel-writers say Peter was, along with James and John, one of a small inner group of disciples who shared the most intimate moments of Jesus' life. At Caesarea Philippi Peter confessed his faith that Jesus was the Christ, but then denied three times that he

> *You are Peter, and on this rock I will build my Church, and the gates of Hades will not overcome it. I will give you the keys of the kingdom of heaven; whatever you bind on earth will be bound in heaven, and whatever you loose on earth will be loosed in heaven.*
>
> MATTHEW 16:18–19

Peter is known as the 'Prince of Apostles'. He is usually shown as an old man, with a flowing beard, dressed in a white mantle and a blue tunic, and holding in his hand a book of scrolls. His symbols are a key and a sword.

knew Jesus just before the crucifixion.

On the Day of Pentecost Peter made a powerful speech in which he declared that Jesus had risen from the dead and was God's chosen Messiah. He was the greatest miracle-worker among the apostles; even his shadow could lead to healing. He opened up the Church to non-Jews (Gentiles) by admitting the Roman Cornelius after receiving a vision from heaven, and he played a central role in the Council of Jerusalem in 51 CE. Here, the position of non-Jews in the Church was debated and a compromise was reached. It seems, however, that Peter was unhappy about the compromise so the mantle of Church leadership passed to Paul.

Peter in the Church

Peter is a significant figure in the history and development of

Peter is often portrayed carrying the keys to the kingdom of heaven as a consequence of Jesus' prophecy about him. *St Peter* by the Master of the Palazzo Venezia Madonna (active mid-14th century).

THE DEATH OF PETER

If Peter did spend any time as Bishop of Rome we have no independent evidence of it. However, a strong tradition maintains that he was finally crucified upside down during the Neronian persecution of Christians in 64–68 CE, which may also have brought about the death of Paul.

the Catholic Church. This stems from the Church's belief that he was the first Bishop of Rome, or Pope, and that the special authority given to him by Jesus has been passed down to each successive holder of that post.

> *[In the Cornelius–Peter episode]*
> *what we often overlook is that*
> *Peter too was converted. It was a*
> *rude shock to him, as it was to*
> *Jonah before him, that God's grace*
> *knows no bounds and extends to*
> *outsiders who are not normally*
> *recipients of such love.*
>
> R.S. SUGIRTHARAJAH,
> SRI LANKAN THEOLOGIAN

Paul

No one has had a greater impact on the Christian Church in the last 2,000 years than Paul. He was an indefatigable traveller and missionary, responsible for establishing many churches as well as writing many letters which set the course for Christian belief and theology.

According to the Acts of the Apostles the first Christian martyr was Stephen. Stephen was stoned to death in the presence of Saul of Tarsus who was leading the early persecution of the Christians. Saul was a Pharisaic Jew, a strict observer of the Jewish law, a student of the great Jewish rabbi Gamaliel and a Roman citizen. The High Priest permitted him to travel to Damascus and round up Christians but during the journey Saul encountered Christ himself. He was blinded by a great light from heaven, which was stronger than the sun, and he heard the voice of Jesus asking why he, Saul, was persecuting the Church. After three days in Damascus Saul's sight was restored and he was baptized straight away. He then began to preach that Jesus was the Son of God. Around this time Saul became known as Paul.

The dramatic moment when Saul encountered Jesus is captured in this illustration for a French Book of Hours, Paris, 1407.

Paul's legacy

The enormous legacy that Paul bequeathed to the Church has been felt in three ways – through his missionary work, church planting and letter writing:

◆ Around 45 CE Paul set out with Barnabas to undertake his first journey as a Christian missionary. He made two later journeys around the Mediterranean Sea before returning to Jerusalem in 58 CE.

◆ The Christian Church grew very quickly in Paul's time. Once Paul had visited an area and preached there, he often established new churches to look after the converts. Because most of these converts came from pagan backgrounds they had little knowledge of the Christian faith, so Paul spent

Legend has it that Paul was beheaded in Rome after converting one of Emperor Nero's favourite concubines to Christianity. Legend also says that milk rather than blood flowed from his veins.

much of his time teaching them.

◆ Paul wrote many letters, called epistles, both to churches and to individual Christians. Many of these are preserved in the New Testament, although not all of those that bear his name actually came from his pen. Some of Paul's epistles, such as his letter to the Romans, are long and theologically complex, while others, such as his letter Philemon, are very brief. Paul's letters were saved and, because of his unrivalled reputation, sent around to as many churches as possible. This is why the Christian Church of the time bore the indelible imprint of Paul the apostle.

For two years Paul lived in Ephesus and daily debated and taught about the kingdom of God. The theatre at Ephesus was the scene of a riot instigated by silversmiths who feared a drop in profits as citizens converted to Christianity and no longer wanted to buy their silver models of the temple of Artemis.

When St Paul's voice was raised to preach the gospel to all nations, it was like a great clap of thunder up above. His preaching was a blazing fire, carrying all before it. It was the sun rising in full glory. Unbelief was consumed by it, wrong beliefs fled away, and the truth was made manifest like a great candle lighting the whole world with its bright flame.

BERNADINE OF SIENA (1380–1444), ITALIAN FRANCISCAN

The care and creativity invested in copies of the Gospels during Europe's Dark Ages is well illustrated in this beautifully constructed initial letter from the *Book of Kells.*

Many Christians believe the Bible to be the word of God, divinely inspired. The Eastern Orthodox Church goes even further and claims that 'the Gospel is not just Holy Scripture but also a symbol of Divine Wisdom and an image of Christ Himself'. The Bible is comprised of two parts: the Old Testament – the Jewish scriptures – which represents to Christians God's first covenant with the human race; and the New Testament, the covenant of Jesus Christ, in whom the promises of God to Israel are fulfilled.

The 39 books of the Old Testament are the same as those in the Jewish scriptures but the books are in a different order. In the Jewish scriptures they are divided into books of the Law, books of the Prophets and books of the Writings.

The 27 books of the New Testament were composed in the decades following the death of Jesus. They include the four Gospels, the Acts of the Apostles and many letters written by Paul and other Christian leaders to young churches and Christian believers.

Roman Catholic Old Testaments also include some later Jewish books of secondary importance. These books sometimes appear in a separate section in Protestant Bibles known as the Apocrypha.

Christians view the Bible in different ways. For many the Bible is entirely revelation: every word is inspired by God, so thought to be

> *In fact, there is no rupture, but continuity between what was revealed to the people of God in the past and the breath of the Spirit that accompanies the reading of the Bible within faith communities today.*
>
> TEREZA CAVALCANTI,
> BRAZILIAN UNIVERSITY TEACHER

inerrant. Others believe the Bible teaches eternal truths about God and the spiritual search but they are open to questions which arise about its factual accuracy.

THE BIBLE

Contents

The Old Testament

The Christian Bible is unique among the world's holy books because it incorporates the entire scriptures of another religion – Judaism. The name Christians gave these scriptures – the Old Testament – implies that their main purpose was to point to the events covered in the New Testament.

The books of the Old Testament trace God's plan for humankind from the creation of the world right through to the time when his people, the Israelites, were anticipating the coming of their Messiah.

The story begins

Genesis is the first book of the Old Testament – a book of beginnings. It starts with chapters covering creation, Adam and Eve and Noah's ark. These are widely regarded as myth, which simply means that while they may not yield literal truths their spiritual value is considerable. What they say about God and humanity rings true.

The rest of Genesis tells the story of Abraham and his

Moses Receives Tablets of the Ten Commandments on Mount Sinai, a 16th-century fresco in the Sucevita Monastery, Moldova, Romania.

descendants, and of the covenant that God made with him, setting the scene for the remainder of the Old Testament.

The next four books of the Old Testament concern Moses, whom God chose to lead the Israelites out of slavery in Egypt. At this point God made the Israelites into a nation, Israel, for the first time. He gave them many laws, including the Ten Commandments, the most influential law code in history and led them to the Promised Land of Canaan. He made a fresh covenant with them, promising that if they served him then he would provide them with all they needed.

> *Ever since you were a child, you have known the Holy Scriptures, which are able to give you the wisdom that leads to salvation through faith in Christ Jesus. All Scripture is inspired by God and is useful for teaching the truth, rebuking error, correcting faults, and giving instruction for right living.*
>
> 2 TIMOTHY 3:15–16

Prophets and kings

The remainder of the Old Testament is a continuous story of God's stormy relationship with the Jewish people, Israel. This relationship is described in a series of 'histories', including the books of Joshua, Kings and Nehemiah, while the books of the Prophets, including Isaiah, Ezekiel and Malachi, tell how God pleaded with his chosen people time and time again to return to serving him. A succession of kings, good

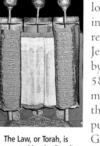

The Law, or Torah, is represented by the first five books of the Christian Bible.

and bad, including David and Solomon, provided leadership which often left a lot to be desired. Then one part of the kingdom was lost to the Assyrians in 721 BCE and the remainder fell when Jerusalem was sacked by the Babylonians in 586 BCE. The prophets made it clear that the Jews were being punished for ignoring God's laws and for following the path of idolatry.

The Old Testament also contains the beautiful devotional literature of the book of Psalms and the deeply thoughtful books of Proverbs, Ecclesiastes and Job.

The New Testament

The New Testament contains the documents upon which the Christian faith is founded – the historical documents of the Gospels and the Acts of the Apostles and the letters written by early Christian leaders, especially Paul.

The writings in the New Testament can be divided into four groups.

The Gospels

The four Gospels – Matthew, Mark, Luke and John – tell the story of Jesus. Three of them – Matthew, Mark and Luke – are called the Synoptic Gospels because they share so much of their material and take a similar approach to the events they are describing. The earliest of these, Mark, was written about 65 CE, about the time that Peter and Paul were being martyred, with the other two following by about 80 CE. The fourth Gospel, John's, takes a very different approach and was written some time later.

The Acts of the Apostles

The Acts of the Apostles describes the history of the early Christian Church during the first few years of its existence. It was written by Luke, sometime travelling companion of Paul and the author of a Gospel. The story moves from the ascension of Jesus into heaven, through the outpouring of the Holy Spirit on the Day of Pentecost, to the imprisonment of Paul in Rome around 62 CE. At the book's heart are the three missionary journeys that Paul made around the Roman empire, marking a time of great expansion for the fledgling Christian Church.

The epistles or letters

Many New Testament epistles are attributed to the apostle Paul, although we cannot be sure just how many of them he actually wrote. We do know, however, that his letters are the earliest documents in the New

The 'canonical books' (the books included in the New Testament) were the books which established 'the rule of faith', as distinct from other books which might be good but did not have the same authority.

OWEN CHADWICK,
CHURCH HISTORIAN

> *The two classes of people who are my particular friends in the Gospels are the crooks and the crocks… Our weakness and our sinfulness are our greatest claims on the mercy of God.*
>
> CHARLES HANDY,
> BRITISH ECONOMIST AND
> MANAGEMENT CONSULTANT

Testament, with all of them having been completed before the first Gospel was written. Other epistles were written by such early Church leaders as Peter, James and John. The majority of these letters set out to explain the significance of the death and resurrection of Jesus – and their relevance to everyday Christian experience.

The book of Revelation

Revelation, the last book in the Bible, is a highly symbolic account of the end of the world, as witnessed by John in a vision on the island of Patmos.

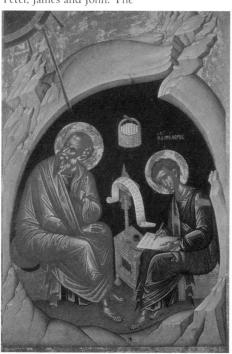

The Gospels of Matthew, Mark and Luke share much common material, but each writer brought his own distinctive style and emphasis to his text.

The Canon

Nearly all the books of the Old and New Testaments were accepted as authoritative long before they were officially included in their respective canons. Once included they were held as the standard by which all matters of belief and behaviour should be judged.

Every major religion has its own collection of holy scriptures, which members of that faith accept as authoritative. The collection itself is called a canon, from the Greek word meaning 'measuring rod'. Thus the books of the Bible provide a benchmark for Christian practice and doctrine.

The canon of the Christian scriptures covers all 66 books in the Bible. These books were originally included because their spiritual value was recognized and treasured.

The Old Testament

Most of the books recognized by Jews as authoritative had been accepted as such by the time of Jesus. Whenever the scriptures are referred to in the New Testament, the Jewish or Hebrew scriptures are meant. As most of the early Christians were Jews they would have been familiar with these scriptures. A final stamp of approval was given to the books in the Jewish canon at the Synod of Jamnia in 90 CE. The term 'Old Testament', however, does not seem to have been in general usage until around 170 CE.

A number of later Jewish works, written in Greek rather than in Hebrew, are included in Roman Catholic editions of the

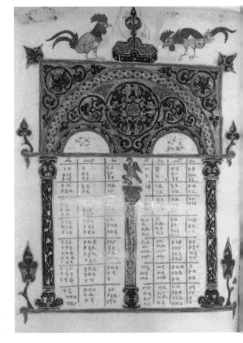

> *Canon: the determination of books which have authority in a religion, either because they are believed to be inspired or revealed, or because they have been so designated. In Christianity... the decision about which books were to be included or excluded was a long process.*
>
> OXFORD DICTIONARY
> OF WORLD RELIGIONS

Old Testament. These are sometimes distinguished as 'deuterocanonical' – of lesser importance than the Hebrew scriptures. Protestant Bibles do not include these works in the Old Testament, but they are sometimes printed in a separate section, known as the Apocrypha.

The New Testament

The New Testament writers frequently quoted from the Jewish scriptures as they were anxious to show that much of what happened to Jesus was foretold by these earlier authors. They were then able to present Jesus as the Messiah who fulfilled all that was predicted and anticipated by the Jewish prophets of old.

The letters written by Paul, Peter, John and other Church leaders in the decades following the death of Jesus may have had

a specific destination but they were circulated much more widely than this and highly prized. The apostles, after all, were the only people with first-hand experience of Jesus. Paul, the most prolific apostle, may not have been an original disciple but, due to his dramatic conversion on the Damascus Road, was an 'ex officio' member of the group.

Individuals and congregations began to collect the different books and letters that were circulating and these were soon united in an 'unofficial' Bible. Justin Martyr (c. 100–c. 165) was the first to speak of the 'New Testament'. By the end of the second century most of the books that are in the New Testament today had been accepted by the Church as divinely inspired. In 367 CE Athanasius, a respected Church leader, set out his own canon which contained 27 books. The same canon was confirmed at the Synod of Carthage in 397 CE, although it was not until the 16th century, at the Council of Trent, that the Roman Catholic Church officially accepted the canon of the Christian Bible.

The spiritual authority, or otherwise, of books determined whether or not they were included in the canon. A Byzantine illumination of a canon table from *Codex Ebnerianus*, Constantinople, early 12th century.

God's Word

The Reformed Churches were largely established on the belief that authority resides solely in the Bible. Others, though, believe that authority lies within the Church and its traditions, with the Bible providing a key source of divine inspiration.

Christians assign divine authority to the Bible because they believe it had a divine origin. Paul wrote of the scriptures as being 'God-breathed', adding that no one could know anything about God unless God had chosen to reveal it.

Authority

Christians across the traditions believe that the final authority for their beliefs and actions can come from three different, but related, sources: the Bible, the Church and the traditions of the Church.

Protestants attach supreme authority to the teachings of the Bible. Any other authority can only be accepted when it is in accord with scripture. This most fundamental of teachings from the Reformation has remained the cornerstone of Reformed Churches ever since.

Roman Catholics believe that all three sources have been used by the Holy Spirit to guide and direct Catholic believers over the centuries with the Church speaking through the Pope.

In the Eastern Orthodox Church it is Church tradition, rather than the Pope, which is the main source of authority alongside the Bible.

The Bible as God's word

The phrase 'the word of God' is deeply rooted in Christian worship. Very often the Bible readings which form an integral part of that worship are introduced or ended with a reference to 'God's word'. The meaning of the phrase, however, is difficult to pin down as it clearly means different things across the various traditions:

> *It is one thing to be told that the Bible has authority because it is divinely inspired, and another thing to feel one's heart leap out and grasp its truth.*
>
> LESLIE WEATHERHEAD,
> BRITISH METHODIST MINISTER

A page from *Codex Siniaticus*, a fourth-century Greek Bible, showing the text of the 21st chapter of John's Gospel.

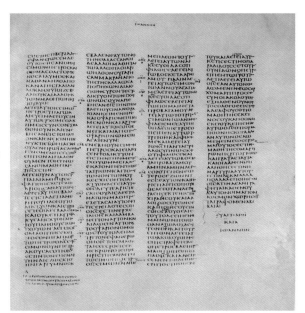

◆ To the fundamentalist it means that God spoke and his words were recorded in the Bible, so the holy book is inerrant, in other words, without error. This makes the words of the Bible God's direct word to human beings in its entirety.

◆ To the evangelical it means that the words of God were transmitted directly to human beings who recorded them – sometimes imperfectly – in their own words. Thus the reader can glimpse the individual personalities of the writers through their writing, but the authority of the Bible, God's word cannot be doubted.

◆ To the liberal it means that the writers of the books were influenced by the attitudes and ideas of their time, many of which would not be accepted today. The Bible contains the words of God but is not God's word in its entirety.

Christians, then, do not agree on exactly how the Bible should be understood. They do agree, however, that it should have a prominent and valued place in their worship.

Using the Bible

The Bible is a great source of inspiration, teaching and comfort for Christian believers and, as such, it plays a central part in both public and private worship. Evangelicals, in particular, place a strong emphasis on the need to grow in a knowledge and understanding of the Bible's teaching.

Passages from the Bible are read in almost all Christian services as well as providing the basis for sermons given by priests, ministers and laypeople. These sermons are an important part of almost all church services although Protestants tend to attach greater importance to them than other Churches.

The sermon in a service provides an opportunity for some part of the Bible to be expounded.

The Bible in public worship
Both the Anglican and Roman Catholic Churches have a systematic programme for the public reading of most of the Bible over a period of time – the readings are set down in a lectionary. In most Anglican and Roman Catholic services there are three readings from the Bible – from the Old Testament, the Epistles and the Gospels. The readings from the Old Testament and one of the Epistles is usually taken by a member of the congregation but the one from the Gospels is taken by the priest to underline its importance. In Roman

It is clear from this process of gaining distance and coming closer that in Latin America the Bible is not read as an intellectual or academic exercise; it is read with the goal of giving meaning to our lives today.

ELSA TAMEZ,
MEXICAN METHODIST THEOLOGIAN

Catholic, Eastern Orthodox and some High Anglican churches the Gospels are carried in procession to the middle of the church before the passage is read since they are the foundational documents of the Christian faith.

Many Churches also have mid-week meetings at which the Bible is studied and taught. Some of these sessions are closely linked with forthcoming festivals such as Christmas and Easter but often they provide an opportunity for some serious and systematic Bible study throughout the year.

Private Bible reading
Most Christians also spend some time regularly reading the Bible on their own. A familiarity with the Bible, and its contents, is seen as being very important for personal growth in the spiritual life. Study notes are available, at different levels, to explain the passages and suggest ways in which the Bible reading might be carried out systematically. Often Christians meet together in small house groups to study the Bible and discuss with each other what it has to say.

Group Bible study. Christians today usually spend some time studying the Bible, either on their own or in a church group.

In the contemporary world there is huge diversity among Christians. However, there remain fundamental beliefs to which the majority adhere – such as faith in one God, who expresses himself in the world as a Trinity: Father, Son and Holy Spirit, and the belief that Jesus is the Son of God, that through his death and resurrection he has conquered sin and given all people the chance to be forgiven by and reconciled with God.

Many Christians see the life of Jesus as a model for moral and ethical behaviour, and they take heart from his full identification with human beings. Because of Christ's resurrection Christians believe in the final resurrection of the body which will happen when Jesus returns to earth (the Second Coming).

A mass of crosses covering a hillside in Lithuania.

In the early centuries of the Christian Church several common statements of belief, called Creeds, were drawn up. Although this was attempting to define the indefinable, it was felt necessary that 'orthodox' faith should be articulated – if only to marginalize those who held unorthodox views. Probably the oldest and simplest of these Creeds is one first recorded in 390 CE – the Apostles' Creed.

God does not occupy an Olympian fastness, remote from us. He has this deep, deep solidarity with us. God became a human being, a baby. God was hungry. God was tired, God suffered and died. God is there with us.

DESMOND TUTU,
SOUTH AFRICAN CHRISTIAN LEADER

CHRISTIAN BELIEFS

Contents

The Trinity

Central to the Christian faith is the unfathomable mystery of the Trinity — the belief that God is three persons in one — God the Father, God the Son and God the Holy Spirit.

When St Patrick (c. 390–c. 461) was trying to explain basic Christian beliefs to his converts in Ireland he is said to have picked up a shamrock to describe the Trinity. Just as the shamrock has a leaf with three equal parts, he told them, so there are three equal and distinct persons in the Trinity who are integral to each other — three in one and one in three.

One leaf or three? St Patrick used a shamrock to help illustrate the concept of God who is one in substance, but appears as three distinct persons.

Three in one

The Trinity is not spelled out as such in the Bible although there are passages in which there is a threefold pattern. The story of Jesus' baptism, for instance, brings together each member of the Trinity: Jesus hears the voice of God from heaven and receives the Holy Spirit to empower him for his forthcoming ministry. At the end of his life on earth Jesus instructed his disciples to baptize new converts in the name of 'the Father, and of the Son and of the Holy Spirit'.

It was against this background that the early Creeds were formulated. In them it was stressed that although the three parts of the Trinity work in different ways they all work together:

◆ God the Father is the Creator of all things.
◆ God the Son is the Saviour and Redeemer who gives life to all.
◆ God the Holy Spirit is the Sanctifier, the One who makes holy.

The Creator, the Redeemer and the Sanctifier are not three gods

The Trinity is at the heart of the Christian faith, yet it remains a mystery which defies human understanding. *The Trinity* by Jacopo di Cione (active c. 1362, died 1398/1400).

> *The Holy Trinity, pervading all men from first to last, from head to foot, binds them all together.*
>
> SIMEON THE NEW THEOLOGIAN (949–1022), MONK AND MYSTIC OF THE EASTERN CHURCH

but one God working in three distinct ways. The Christian faith, like the Jewish faith out of which it grew, is strictly monotheistic, committed to belief in one God. Christians and Jews alike share the certainty of the *Shema* – 'Hear, O Israel: The Lord our God, the Lord is one.'

Because of the problems with talking about three persons in a monotheistic context some modern Christians have spoken of three minds, spirits or energies which are all part of the same God and exist in harmony: God the Father loving God the Son with the Holy Spirit as the force that unites them. Other Christians think it is easier to speak of God having three roles: he is in himself Father, Son and Spirit.

The Incarnation

Christians believe in the incarnation – that Jesus, the Son of God, became fully human yet at the same time retained all of his divine nature. The corollary of this is that when Jesus was on the cross it was God himself who was suffering.

'I believe in Jesus Christ, [God's] only Son, our Lord.' This statement from the Apostles' Creed perfectly encapsulates the Christian belief that Jesus is, above all else, God's Son.

The Son of God

Applied to God the term 'son' must be understood as a metaphor indicating that Jesus shared God's nature, he was human and divine and he gave the fullest possible expression to the love that God has for humanity. Jesus was God incarnate.

The Son of God came down to earth and endured its pain and suffering with humble obedience. He was the perfect example of God's destiny and purpose for humankind.

The lordship of Christ

The Apostles' Creed speaks of 'our Lord' and this phrase is the key to understanding the incarnation of Jesus. For Christians the word 'Lord',

He always had the nature of God, but he did not think that by force he should try to remain equal with God. Instead of this, of his own free will he gave up all he had and took the nature of a servant. He became like a human being and appeared in human likeness. He was humble and walked the path of obedience all the way to death – his death on the cross. For this reason God raised him to the highest place above and gave him the name that is greater than any other name.

PHILIPPIANS 2:6–9

often used in both Old and New Testaments, does not refer to an earthly king, full of power and majesty, with all the trappings of royalty. Instead, the true Lord is Jesus of Nazareth, the servant of humanity. It was God himself who became man in Jesus, took on human flesh and was both truly human and fully divine. This is yet another mystery of Christianity, supported by certain episodes in the New Testament. Thomas Aquinas (c. 1225–74), the Catholic philosopher, stated that the incarnation of Jesus meant

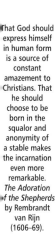

That God should express himself in human form is a source of constant amazement to Christians. That he should choose to be born in the squalor and anonymity of a stable makes the incarnation even more remarkable. *The Adoration of the Shepherds* by Rembrandt van Rijn (1606–69).

Too bored to think, too proud to pray, too timid to leave what we are used to doing, we have shut ourselves behind our standard roses; we love ourselves only and our neighbours no longer. As for the Incarnation, that is a fairy story for children, if we think it healthy for children to be told fairy stories.

JOHN BETJEMAN,
ENGLISH POET

that God became human and human beings became sharers in the divine nature.

The Atonement

The atonement indicates humanity's reunion with God through the life, suffering, death and resurrection of Jesus Christ.

It is the crucifixion and resurrection of Jesus, rather than his incarnation, which mainly occupy the thoughts of the New Testament writers, especially Paul.

The death of Jesus

About 30 per cent of the Gospel narrative is devoted to the last week in the life of Jesus, leading up to his crucifixion. Paul's major concern in his letters was to explain the significance of Jesus' death and to do this he used several 'pictures':

◆ He compares Jesus to the innocent lamb sacrificed each year at Passover. Jews believed that by shedding the blood of a

The Old Testament offerings of unblemished lambs reminded the people how their sins had offended a holy God. But it was not until the sacrificial death of Jesus that sins were dealt with once and for all. *The Bound Lamb* (*Agnus Dei*) by Francisco de Zurbaran (1598–1664).

> *If Christ has not been raised, your faith is futile; you are still in your sins. Then those also who have fallen asleep in Christ are lost. If only for this life we have hope in Christ, we are to be pitied more than all men. But Christ has indeed been raised from the dead.*
>
> 1 CORINTHIANS 15:17–20

perfect lamb their sins would be forgiven by God. The sacrifice acted as their payment to God, demonstrating the cost of their sin. But it had to be offered each year, whereas Jesus' sacrifice atoned for the sins of the world once and for all.

◆ He describes how the death of Jesus brought about the final defeat of the powers of evil. Jesus' ministry was a constant battle against these powers but his death and return to life marked his ultimate victory over them. As a result all human beings can be liberated from the power of sin and death through faith in Jesus.

◆ He explains how the death of Jesus redeemed humanity. Through its sinful behaviour the human race had effectively 'sold' itself to Satan but Jesus had paid the necessary price to 'buy it back'. When Jesus died on the cross he, who was without sin,

took on every single sin of every single person in the world. That sin died with him and was buried, but Jesus returned to life, bringing with him the hope of eternal life for all.

Paul took most of these images from his Jewish background. Together they present the death of Jesus as an 'at-one-ment', a unification of a holy God and sinful humanity.

The resurrection of Jesus

Christians believe that the resurrection of Jesus completes all that he accomplished on the cross. Paul stated unequivocally that Jesus' death would have been meaningless unless God had brought him back to life. The resurrection sets God's seal on everything: if the evil powers could not keep the Son of God sealed in the tomb they cannot have ultimate power over human beings either.

The Holy Spirit

Christians believe that the Holy Spirit is the third person of the Trinity and one with the God the Father and God the Son – co-equal and co-eternal.

The Holy Spirit is the power of God active in the world, just as Jesus was, carrying out the will of the Father. In the New Testament the Holy Spirit is closely identified with Jesus; Jesus promised him to his disciples and so he came to them on the Day of Pentecost. The description of the Spirit's arrival in the Acts of the Apostles underlines the power felt at his coming: 'a sound like the blowing of a violent wind'. Everyone present was amazed at this display of God's power, which drew people towards his divine love.

The Holy Spirit empowered the early Christians as they began

Throughout Christian history the Holy Spirit has been represented by a dove – the form in which he appeared at Jesus' baptism. *The Baptism of Christ* (before 526, cupola mosaic), Baptistery of Arians.

to spread the gospel of Christ and turn the world upside down. They were filled with the love of God. However, many thought that those who received the Spirit on the Day of Pentecost were drunk because of the way they were behaving, speaking in foreign tongues.

> *God has poured out his love into our hearts by the Holy Spirit, whom he has given us... The Spirit helps us in our weakness. We do not know what we ought to pray, but the Spirit himself intercedes for us with groans that words cannot express.*
>
> ROMANS 5:5; 8:26

THE GIFTS OF THE SPIRIT

In the early Church gifts given by the Holy Spirit were believed to strengthen the community and make its witness more effective in the world. These gifts included performing miracles, healing, prophecy, speaking in tongues, interpreting strange tongues and teaching. The same gifts were apparent during the latter half of the 20th century through the Pentecostal Church and the charismatic movement.

> *But the fruit of the Spirit is love, joy, peace, patience, kindness, goodness, faithfulness, gentleness, self-control; against such there is no law.*
>
> GALATIANS 5:22–23

The body of Christ

John the Baptist knew that while he baptized people with water, Jesus would baptize them in the Holy Spirit. This is a much more powerful baptism since it marks each person's entry into new life, a sharing of the life of God. Part of this new life involved becoming a member of the Christian community, the body of Christ, the Church. Those who believed were baptized into this body with the words, 'I baptize you in the name of the Father, and of the Son and of the Holy Spirit.' The Church today remains the body of Christ and baptism in the name of the Holy Trinity is the path most people follow to join it.

The Creeds

A creed is a statement of belief. Remnants of the first Creeds can be found in the New Testament, but only two of them – the Apostles' Creed and the Nicene Creed – have played an important part in Christian worship.

To discover the origins of the Creeds, we have to go back to the New Testament. Early Christians used various forms of words to teach young converts about the new faith. The earliest of these have left their mark in the writings of Paul and probably included 'Jesus is Lord' and 'God raised the Lord Jesus from the dead.'

To begin with, these formulae of faith were only used within small communities, but as the Christian leaders travelled more widely to spread the gospel so their use spread as well. They were particularly useful for teaching people who had come forwards for baptism. As a way of preparing candidates for this step of faith the bishop would 'hand out' the short statements, commenting on them phrase by phrase. Then, during the baptism ceremony, the converts would 'give the Creeds back', as a way of expressing their own personal commitment to Christ.

The value of the Creeds

During the early centuries of the Church's existence there were people who, from time to time, preached something different from the Church leaders. Such believers were called 'heretics' and their unorthodox views could be identified by comparison with the Creeds. Then, if necessary, the heretics could be expelled from the Church. The Roman Catholic and Anglican Churches accept

I believe in God, the Father Almighty, Creator of heaven and earth. I believe in Jesus Christ, his only Son, our Lord. He was conceived by the power of the Holy Spirit and born of the Virgin Mary. He suffered under Pontius Pilate, was crucified, died and was buried. He descended to the dead. On the third day he rose again. He ascended into heaven, and is seated on the right hand of God the Father. He will come again to judge the living and the dead. I believe in the Holy Spirit, the holy, catholic Church, the communion of saints, the forgiveness of sins, the resurrection of the body and the life everlasting. Amen.

THE APOSTLES' CREED

There is a legend that the 12 apostles of Jesus came together and listed the most important elements of belief – the Apostles' Creed. We now know there is no truth behind this legend; it was invented to give that Creed as much authority as possible.

three Creeds – the Athanasian Creed, the Apostles' Creed and the Nicene Creed – although the Athanasian Creed is considered too long and prescriptive to be used widely. While the roots of the Apostles' Creed may lie in the second century, it only appeared in its present form in the 11th century. The Nicene Creed was issued by a council of bishops meeting in Nicea in 325 CE. It is used in the Eucharist services of Roman Catholic, Anglican and Eastern Orthodox Churches, as well as in Orthodox baptism services.

From its earliest time the Christian Church recognized the death of Jesus as central to their faith and this is reflected in the Creeds. *The Man of Sorrows as the Image of Pity* (Venetian, 14th century).

The Church

The New Testament Church was a gathering of people,
a community of believers who were united in their love
of Jesus and who sought to share everything together.
Throughout history the Church has been made up of
those trying to continue Christ's work on earth.

Some people see the
church as a building where
Christians gather for worship.
Others think of it as an
institution where rites such
as baptisms, weddings and
funerals are conducted.
However, the New Testament
makes it clear that the Church
is *people*. The Greek word for
Church, used in the New
Testament, means 'a called-out
gathering'. The Church is the
people of God, called out to
know, love and serve him.

Different images are used
in the New Testament to
describe the Church. For
example, the Church is
portrayed as the 'body of
Christ', a growing organism
with Christ as its head. It is
also depicted as the 'bride of
Christ', vitally connected to
him. Above all the Church is
about people of all different
kinds, with many imperfections
and limitations. The one thing
that unites them is Christ.

The Church is described in
the Nicene Creed as:

◆ one: there may be many
different Churches but
underlying the divisions
is a strong spiritual unity.
◆ holy: the word 'holy' means

THE CHALLENGE TO CHURCHES IN THE WEST

Since the latter part of the 20th century,
traditional Churches in the West have been
suffering from severe numerical decline. In
recent years, this drift away from organized
Christianity has been accompanied by a
strong interest in what is known as New
Age spirituality or the New Spirituality. Many
people are searching for new forms of spiritual
fulfilment and not finding it in the institutional
Churches, whose spiritual life often seems dry
and unattractive. The New Age movement is
an umbrella term for many different interests,
ranging from creation-centred mysticism through
various forms of self-fulfilment therapies to
occult practices. The challenge facing Western
Churches is immense and contrasts starkly with
the vibrant faith evident in many other parts
of the world, where Christianity seems to be
a much more intrinsic part of people's lives.

The Church is the people of God. Teaching helps believers of all ages understand what the Christian faith is all about.

Only three Councils of the Catholic Church have been called since the 16th century: the Council of Trent (1545–63), the First Vatican Council (1869–70) and the Second Vatican Council (1962–65).

'set apart from everything else' and in this sense God is holy. The Church is the material presence of Christ on earth, created to continue the work he began.

◆ catholic: the worldwide community of the Church must be universal, embracing people of different cultures and backgrounds.

◆ apostolic: the Church was created during the time of the apostles and their authority has been handed down through the line of bishops to the present time. Bishops today have the same role as the apostles of old — preaching, teaching and administering sacraments such as baptism and Communion.

Not all denominations recognize the Creeds or believe in the apostolic succession of bishops, and many Reformed Churches accept the Bible as the only form of authority.

> *The Church... cannot be seen simply as the company of believers who have had spiritual experiences. It is the company of those whose lives are perceived to have the quality of Christ-in-his-struggle-against-human-bondage. It is thus the company of liberators, or it is not the Church.*
>
> SABELO NTWASA,
> SOUTH AFRICAN BLACK THEOLOGIAN

The Virgin Mary

Veneration of Mary has come more from the grass roots of the Church than from its leaders. Drawings of Mary have been found in the catacombs of Rome, where the early Christians met, and explicit devotion to her was well developed by the third or fourth century CE. Mary is particularly adored by Roman Catholics, Eastern Orthodoxy and High Anglicans.

Mary plays a prominent part in the birth narratives found in the first two chapters of Matthew's Gospel and of Luke's Gospel. However, although Mary is mentioned several times later on in the Gospels, she has largely moved to the background. Only John's Gospel mentions her keeping vigil at the foot of the cross of Jesus.

Queen of Heaven

Most Christians believe that Jesus did not have a human father, but was conceived in Mary's womb by the Holy Spirit. This belief is known as the virgin birth. Roman Catholics believe that Mary's obedience in accepting the role of bearing Jesus, the Son of God, marks her out as the

The veneration of Mary remains a strong feature of Eastern Orthodox Christianity. A Russian believer parades an icon of Mary through the streets of Moscow.

supreme example for all Christians to follow. Her faith and trust in God make her the first of all the saints.

Orthodox tradition calls Mary *Theotokos*, meaning 'God-bearer', since it was through her

'Queen of Heaven' and direct their prayers to God through her as their intermediary.

Beliefs about Mary

The Roman Catholic Church holds three specific beliefs about Mary:

◆ She was 'immaculately conceived'. Since the 15th century the Catholic Church has maintained that Mary was born without 'original sin' (the sin which it is believed Adam and Eve brought into the world and handed down to every member of humankind) and so must have been conceived differently from every other human being. This belief was accepted officially by the Catholic Church in 1854.

◆ Mary was a virgin when Jesus was conceived and she remained a virgin throughout her life – the perpetual virginity of Mary.

◆ She was transferred to heaven, body and soul, at the end of her life without dying. This belief is known as the assumption of the Virgin and is shared by Catholic and Orthodox Christians. Although it has been part of the Orthodox Church's teaching for centuries, it only became official Catholic doctrine in 1950.

APPEARANCES OF MARY

Visions of Mary have been common throughout Christian history and she is said to have appeared to many believers around the world. For example, it has been claimed that she appeared repeatedly to a young peasant girl called Bernadette at Lourdes in France in the 19th century. A spring that Mary pointed out to Bernadette has been the source of many medically corroborated healings. In 1531 in Guadalupe, Mexico, Mary is said to have appeared to a converted Aztec, Juan Diego. She asked him to have the bishop build a church on the spot. To persuade his bishop Juan filled his cloak with the out-of-season roses to which Mary led him. When he opened his cloak before the bishop, the petals fell away to reveal a striking image of Mary. This picture is now enshrined in a new church and the Virgin of Guadalupe has been declared celestial patroness of the New World.

that the incarnation was able to take place. She gave birth to God himself, who was taking on human flesh. To Orthodox believers Mary is a unique link between the spiritual and the material worlds – between heaven and earth. Roman Catholics recognize the same thing when they speak of Mary as the

Death and Eternal Life

Christian funerals across the denominations reflect the belief that death is not the end; that after death the soul survives while the body awaits resurrection to share in the victory that Christ won over death by his own resurrection.

In the Eastern Orthodox Church, death is viewed as a human tragedy, the result of sin. This sadness is tempered with hope, however, symbolized by the lighting of candles and the sprinkling of incense. In the funeral service everyone is encouraged to look beyond bereavement to the time when everyone will be raised from the grave and death will be finally abolished. Then everyone, the living and the dead, will be reunited in God's kingdom.

Eternal God, the Lord of life, the conqueror of death, our help in every time of trouble, comfort us who mourn, and give us grace, in the presence of death, to worship you, that we may have sure hope of eternal life and be enabled to put our whole trust in your goodness and mercy, through Jesus Christ our Lord. Amen.

FROM THE METHODIST
FUNERAL SERVICE

Prayers for the eventual reception of the dead by God in heaven are offered in both Catholic and Orthodox Churches. Catholics believe in purgatory, a place between earth and heaven in which the soul is purified in preparation

> *Death is the supreme festival on the road to freedom.*
>
> DIETRICH BONHOEFFER (1905–45), GERMAN LUTHERAN PASTOR

for heaven. The amount of time spent there depends on the prayers of those still alive. Such prayers begin on the night before the funeral, when the coffin is left in the church.

Protestants do not believe in purgatory but they do have a strong faith in life after death. In Protestant funeral services, a person's soul is committed to the safe keeping of God as the body is lowered into the grave. The prayers and the Bible readings during the service demonstrate the belief that once a person dies his or her soul is with God in heaven. Everyone then looks forward to the end of time, when all believers will receive a 'new body', similar to the one that Christ had after he had been raised from the dead.

The assurance that death is not the end for Christians comes from the death and resurrection of Jesus. **The Burial of the Dead** *from a French Book of Hours, illuminated by Maître François, Brittany, c. 1460.*

BORN AGAIN

As well as the new life Christians begin when their physical bodies die, the Bible also teaches about a new spiritual life that starts when they become Christians. In John's Gospel, Jesus tells Nicodemus he needs to be 'born of water and the Spirit' in order to enter the kingdom of God. In his letter to the Romans, Paul writes, 'count yourselves dead to sin but alive to God in Christ Jesus'. Paul also writes, in his second letter to the Corinthians, that 'if anyone is in Christ, he is a new creation; the old has gone, the new has come!'

Judgment

God's final judgment of humankind is a theme that runs right through the Bible. When it happens, God the Father will reveal the truth about everyone's life – the good they have done as well as the evil they have inflicted on others.

It is believed this time of judgment will coincide with Christ's return to earth, or Second Coming. The Roman Catholic Church teaches that there is an individual judgment, which takes place after each person's death, and a general judgment, which happens at the Second Coming of Christ.

For many centuries the Christian Church was essentially united. Although there were disagreements over such issues as admitting non-Jews into the Church, these arguments did not disrupt the unity that stemmed from the experience of the apostles on the Day of Pentecost.

Tensions were bubbling beneath the surface, however, as the Eastern and Western branches of the Church developed different patterns of belief and worship. Wide and irreparable divisions appeared in the 11th century when the two parts disagreed over the authority of the Pope and the exact wording of the Nicene Creed. The Western Catholic Church and the Eastern Orthodox Church went their separate ways.

A few centuries later the Catholic Church itself was shaken to its foundations by the Reformation, which resulted in the emergence of

The consecration of an Eastern Orthodox church in Dumbrava, Romania.

the Reformed Church. Then followed a succession of smaller splits as the Anglican Church, the Lutheran Church, the Methodist Church and the Baptist Church, among others, were formed, finally destroying any hope of a completely united Church.

> *The dividedness of the Churches makes it difficult for people to believe in the gospel of Jesus Christ.*
>
> DESMOND TUTU,
> SOUTH AFRICAN CHRISTIAN LEADER

FROM ONE CHURCH TO MANY

Contents

The Great Schism

During the first five centuries of its existence, the Christian Church was under the authority of the Pope in Rome. This was increasingly challenged by the Eastern Churches, centred around Constantinople, leading to a final split between East and West in 1054.

When the Roman empire finally fell early in the fifth century CE, the seat of power in the Christian Church shifted from West to East – from Rome to Constantinople – and the gulf between the Eastern and Western parts of the Church widened into a chasm. Few people in the East could read Latin, the language of the Western Church, while few in the West knew the Greek of the Eastern Church. Levels of education in the East were high among both clergy and laypeople, whereas in the West only the clergy were literate.

> *If the Roman pontiff desires, from the raised throne of his glory, to hurl his mandates at us from on high; if he desires to judge us and even rule over our churches, without asking our advice but at his own pleasure, what kind of fraternity could that be, what kind of parent would he be?*
>
> AN EASTERN BISHOP, 1136

The final split

During the 11th century matters came to a head. Patriarch Keroularios of Constantinople was incensed when Pope Leo IX imposed a new bishop from Sicily on the Eastern Church. The patriarch responded by closing the Western churches in Constantinople and expelling their clergy. The Pope dispatched his representative, Cardinal Humbert de Silva Candida, to meet with the

The Church of Hagia Sophia, Constantinople, scene of the delivery of the papal bull which severed relations between the Catholic and Eastern Orthodox Churches. The building was opened in 537 by Emperor Justinian.

patriarch, but the talks failed and the representative ended up excommunicating the patriarch and his whole church. Then, in July 1054, Cardinal Humbert stormed into the Church of Hagia Sophia in Constantinople and slammed the bull of excommunication down on the high altar – despite the fact that Pope Leo IX, its instigator, had died three months earlier. The break between the Roman Catholic ('universal') Church and the Eastern Orthodox ('right-thinking') Church was complete.

The Roman Catholic and the Orthodox Churches have similar beliefs and ways of worshipping: they both accept the seven sacraments (Communion, baptism, confirmation, penance, holy orders, the anointing of the sick and marriage), have an episcopal church structure under the leadership of bishops and priests, venerate the Virgin Mary, respect the Bible and Church tradition and observe a full calendar of Church festivals and saints' days.

The issue of the supremacy, or otherwise, of the Pope was too fundamental to be ignored, however. The Orthodox Church has always been willing to accord to the Pope a 'primacy of honour' without, at any time, acknowledging his supreme authority in matters of doctrine and belief.

The Roman Catholic Church

The Roman Catholic Church is the world's largest Christian denomination, comprising almost 60 per cent of all Christians. It believes itself to represent the most primitive form of Christianity, which can be traced back to the apostles.

Roman Catholics believe the Pope, the Bishop of Rome, to be the direct successor of the apostle Peter, the first Pope. The Church also holds that all its beliefs are rooted in the teachings of Jesus and his apostles together with the later traditions of the Church. The question of the Pope's authority led to the Great Schism in 1054 and the Reformation of the 16th century.

At the start of the 21st century there is considerable diversity of opinion within the Catholic Church, among both clergy and laypeople. The Second Vatican Council (1962–65), called by Pope John XXIII, did much to promote contacts with other Churches and faiths, and resulted in many changes, but left the core beliefs of the Church untouched. Pope John Paul II, elected in 1978, has travelled widely, but his papacy has been characterized

The name 'Roman Catholic Church' was introduced by non-Catholics to refer to members of the Catholic or Western Church who were under the jurisdiction of the Pope in Rome. The term is a consequence of the Reformation, and came into use at the end of the 16th century.

The inside of Catholic churches has altered little since before the Reformation.

The decisions taken by the Second Vatican council affected the form and nature of worship more than anything else.

by caution and conservatism, leaving many of the hopes of the Second Vatican Council unrealized.

Inside a Catholic church

Catholic churches are full of symbolism. The stoup, just inside the door, holds the holy water which each worshipper uses to make the sign of the cross across their body as they enter the building. The font, also just inside the door, holds the water used during the ceremony of infant baptism, when a child becomes a member of Christ's Church.

Traditionally, the most sacred part of the church, the altar, has stood against the east wall of the church, but the Second Vatican Council decreed that the altar should be brought forwards, so that the priest can conduct the Mass facing the people. The tabernacle, to one side of the altar, holds the reserved sacrament of bread and wine. As the Virgin Mary plays a prominent role in Catholic devotions there is at least one statue of her in the church, while elsewhere votive candles, symbolizing the light of God, are lit by individual worshippers before they offer their prayer requests.

STATIONS OF THE CROSS

Around the walls of a Catholic church there are 14 stations of the cross, which depict the places where Jesus is believed to have stopped on his way to crucifixion. Services during Lent give worshippers the opportunity to visit each station to meditate and assume the mindset of someone actually undertaking a pilgrimage to Jerusalem.

The Eastern Orthodox Church

The Eastern Orthodox Church believes that it, rather than the Roman Catholic Church, represents the most primitive form of Christianity. There are many Orthodox Churches worldwide which take on the name, and many of the characteristics, of their countries of origin.

The main Eastern Orthodox Churches are the Greek, Russian, Armenian, Coptic and Syrian Churches.

Orthodox tradition

The Orthodox Church lays a profound emphasis on tradition. The Holy Tradition refers to revelations of God that have come down through the prophets, the patriarchs and the incarnation itself. This tradition has been upheld throughout the Church's history by the scriptures, the Creed (usually the Apostles' Creed), the teachings of the first seven councils of the early Church, the writings of the early Church fathers and the use of icons. Holy Tradition is believed to be inspired by the Holy Spirit and so has a divine origin.

This heavy reliance on tradition means the Eastern Orthodox Church cannot change; to do so would be an act of treachery to the legacy of the past. This can be seen most clearly in the Church's attitude

THE RUSSIAN ORTHODOX CHURCH

The wars between Russia and the Ottoman Turks from 1697 to 1878 eventually resulted in Russia's expansion. Consequently, Russia had increased prominence in the Orthodox Church, calling itself the 'third Rome'. At this time the Orthodox Church was strong throughout the Slavic and Eastern Mediterranean countries. However, the Russian Orthodox Church was heavily repressed during the Russian Revolution of 1917. Thousands of monasteries and churches were taken over and, in the early 1920s, thousands of priests, nuns and lay Christians were killed. Nevertheless, the Church survived and lived on in the hearts and minds of ordinary believers, until the collapse of the old Russian Communist system in the 1980s and the ensuing change in attitude towards religious freedom. Still, many Russian Orthodox Christians were disenchanted with the official Church and accused it of collaboration with the state. Even today some Russian Orthodox priests prefer to worship in secret than to subject their congregations to the registration requirements of the state and the disapproval of the official Church.

The mystery of Orthodox religion is underlined by the iconostasis, which separates worshippers from the high altar, the symbol of God's presence.

to the Holy Liturgy. The form that this service of Communion takes has survived untouched since the time of St John Chrysostom (c. 347–407), Doctor of the Church and patriarch of Constantinople. Holy Liturgy is celebrated daily in every Orthodox church, as well as on special festivals and feast days, so continues to provide a link with those early days. For Orthodox believers it becomes a 'window into heaven', focusing on the birth, death and resurrection of Jesus.

> *Tradition is the context in which scripture comes alive, the process whereby the truth if scripture is re-experienced by the Church in every generation.*
>
> KALLISTOS (TIMOTHY) WARE,
> GREEK ORTHODOX BISHOP

Inside an Orthodox church

The Orthodox Church relies more heavily on symbolism than any other Church. The four corners of the church building represent the four Gospels, while the dome symbolizes the heavens and the floor the earth. In larger churches a painting of Christ the Pantocrator (ruler of the heavens, the universe and the earth) stretches across the ceiling. The iconostasis, a screen covered with icons, separates the high altar from members of the congregation. The royal doors in the centre of the iconostasis are only opened for the priest to pass through during the Holy Liturgy. Icons are holy pictures that depict Jesus, Mary or the saints and act as an aid to worship.

The Reformation

The Reformation was ignited during the 16th century by Martin Luther in Germany and by John Calvin and Ulrich Zwingli elsewhere in Europe. The linchpin of the movement was the supremacy of the scriptures over all forms of earthly authority.

In the 14th century reformers such as John Wycliffe (c. 1328–84) in England and Jan Hus (c. 1372–1415) in Czechoslovakia had begun to question the authority of the Catholic Church and its corrupt practices. Both men were condemned as heretics but their views were kept alive by many members of the Church.

Martin Luther

Discontentment with the Catholic Church grew during the 15th century and reached a peak in 1517 when Martin Luther (1483–1546), an Augustinian friar working in Wittenburg, Germany, nailed 95 'theses' to the door of the castle church in the town. He criticized the Catholic Church for selling indulgences to raise funds for the rebuilding of St Peter's in Rome. (An indulgence was meant to guarantee a person immediate access to heaven upon death in return for a payment to the Church.) Luther was excommunicated in 1521.

Luther rejected any doctrine or religious practice which could not be shown to have a biblical basis.

> *I wish that the scriptures might be translated into all languages… I long that the farm labourer might sing them as he follows the plough, the weaver hum them to the tune of his shuttle, the traveller beguile the weariness of his journey with their stories.*
>
> DESIDERIUS ERASMUS (1467–1536), DUTCH HUMANIST SCHOLAR

The break-up of Western Christendom was inevitable. In 1529 a group opposed to the suppression of the reformers was labelled the 'Protestants' and the name stuck. The Protestants advocated the authority of scripture over that of any Church or tradition.

The Lutheran Church was based on Luther's teachings and beliefs. Lutheranism reached Denmark and within a short time spread to Norway and Sweden as part of the political reforms which were sweeping those countries.

The Reformation was an assertion of the supremacy of the Bible over every other source of Christian authority. Martin Luther rejected any doctrine or religious practice which could not be shown to have a biblical basis.
Martin Luther by Lucas Cranach the Elder (1472–1553).

John Calvin and Ulrich Zwingli

As Lutheranism spread from Germany to Scandanavia, another form of Protestantism developed in Switzerland.

Known as the Reformed Church, its prime instigators were Ulrich Zwingli (1484–1531) and John Calvin (1509–64). Arguing for the supremacy of the Bible in all matters, Zwingli maintained that such Catholic practices as the veneration of the saints, celibacy, monasticism, indulgences and absolution were all human inventions. In 1533 John Calvin had a spiritual reawakening which led him to sever all his ties with the Catholic Church. He adopted Reformed principles and, after a time in Salzburg, returned to Geneva where he organized local government on

John Calvin broke from the Catholic Church and was instrumental in establishing the Reformed Church in Switzerland. The social and religious life of the city of Geneva was reorganized so that it conformed to biblical principles of government. *Portrait of John Calvin by the Swiss School (17th century).*

the principle that all religious and social life should be under the lordship of Christ. Calvinism grew out of his theology, and proved very influential throughout the Christian Church. Calvin stressed the transcendance of God, the total depravity of human nature and predestination, with the sole source of authority being the scriptures and the Holy Spirit.

The Anglican and Lutheran Churches

The Anglican and the Lutheran Churches are the largest of the Reformed Churches.

The Church of England separated from the Catholic Church in the 16th century, when King Henry VIII became head of the Church instead of the Pope. Under Queen Elizabeth I the Church of England became the established Church in England and this remains the case today.

The Anglican Church

As the Church of England spread its message into other countries, it became known as the Anglican Church. Today this Church has over 70 million members, most notably in Africa and South America.

Although there is a wide diversity of views within the Anglican Church, the Lambeth Conference of 1888 isolated four beliefs which form the bedrock of Anglicanism:

◆ the scriptures contain everything necessary for salvation.
◆ the Apostles' and Nicene Creeds are full statements of Anglican belief.

◆ the Church only recognizes the two sacraments of Communion and baptism.
◆ the episcopate with the historic line of bishops is the only form of Church organization.

Despite being a Reformed Church the Anglican Church generally places a greater emphasis on celebration of the

The English king Henry VIII clashed with the Pope, who would not grant him a divorce. Henry retaliated by declaring himself to be head of the Church in England. *Portrait of Henry VIII* by Hans Holbein the Younger (1497/9–1543).

In North America seven per cent of the population belong to the Lutheran Church. This Church has three major branches in North America: the Evangelical Lutheran Church in America; the Lutheran Church Missouri Synod and the Evangelical Church in Canada. Each of these Churches is the result of many earlier amalgamations.

sacraments than on preaching the Bible. While the focal point in most Reformed churches is the pulpit, in Anglican churches it is the altar. Some Anglican churches have an open Bible on the lectern, however, as a reminder that this is a Reformed Church.

The Lutheran Church

The Lutheran Church originated from the life and works of Martin Luther and is the main form of Protestantism in Germany, Denmark, Norway, Sweden and Iceland. It also spread into the Baltic States and neighbouring countries, as well as reaching the New World, through German and Scandinavian emigration.

The teaching of the Lutheran Church was summed up by Philipp Melanchthon's Augsburg Confession of 1530

and the writings of Luther himself. These affirm the scriptures as the sole rule of faith, the total depravity of human nature and the inability of human beings to please God, the initiative of divine grace which offers salvation to all, and the response of faith as the means of securing that salvation.

Lutheran faith has strong roots in the family. The importance of preaching, the sacraments of Communion and baptism, hymn-singing and Bible reading is reflected in Church worship. The Church has an episcopal ministry, so it is governed by bishops. The Lutheran Church welcomes women priests and has been prominent in the ecumenical movement.

Martin Luther's Latin Bible with his annotations in the margin.

Other Reformed Churches

Since its foundation the Baptist Church has grown into one of the largest Protestant denominations, as has the Methodist Church. The Salvation Army and the Quakers have also been highly influential.

The Baptist Church was started in 1609 when John Smythe led a group of dissidents from London to Amsterdam to set up a Church which offered membership on the basis of the baptism of all believers. The Great Awakening of the 18th century, a series of religious revivals that swept across colonial America, led to a massive expansion of the Baptist Church in New England. There are now 30 million Baptists in America. In the 19th and 20th centuries the Baptist Church became established in Australia, New Zealand, Asia, Africa and South America.

The Baptist Church is firmly evangelical, believing that the Bible is the source of all spiritual authority and that each local church is a 'gathered community' of believers who have followed Jesus through the waters of baptism.

The Methodist Church

The members of the Holy Club formed in 1729 by John and Charles Wesley, among others, which met in Oxford to study the Bible and pray were first called 'Methodists' because of the methodical way they set about their spiritual tasks. The Methodist Church, though, was not set up until after John Wesley's death in 1791. Wesley

The reading and exposition of the Bible feature significantly in Baptist services. Consequently, buildings are laid out in a way that gives prominence to the pulpit. Communion is celebrated regularly, usually with an invitation to gather round the 'Lord's table'.

John Wesley travelled over 250,000 miles in the course of his preaching ministry, which lasted for more than 50 years. Huge numbers of people, particularly among the poor, responded to his message. His preaching radically changed the society of 18th-century Britain. *Portrait of John Wesley* (1766) by Nathaniel Hone (1718–84).

The Salvation Army and the Quakers are the only Churches which do not celebrate any sacraments.

The Quakers

The Quaker movement was begun in the middle of the 17th century and it is based on four religious principles first expounded by George Fox: the light of God (the divine spark) is found in everyone; ministers are unnecessary since each person can wait for God to speak to them; there are no creeds or liturgies in worship; and there are no sacraments since life itself is sacramental.

remained a priest in the Church of England until his death.

Wesley set up classes, under itinerant preachers, to encourage people to live a life of prayer and discipline in the fellowship of the Holy Spirit. He insisted that conversion to Christ must be followed by a life of personal holiness. The necessity of personal conversion and Wesley's classes became features of the Methodist Church.

Music is a prominent aspect of life in the Salvation Army. Singers and musicians feature in open-air services, where hymns are sung and the gospel is preached.

The Salvation Army

The Salvation Army was formed in 1878 by William and Catherine Booth. It has a strong social conscience alongside strict evangelical principles. Organized along semi-military lines Salvation Army members wear a distinctive uniform, sign 'Articles of War' (a statement of Salvationist beliefs and principles) and worship in citadels. The Salvation Army is involved in local community work. It organizes rescue work after natural disasters, takes care of ex-criminals and alcoholics, runs soup kitchens for those living on the streets, finances hospitals, schools and hostels, and runs a very effective tracing service for those reported as missing.

As the Christian Church enters the 21st century it finds, for the first time, that its heartland is no longer in the West. Two out of every three Christians are now found outside the USA and Europe. This is largely due to very effective work carried out by Western Christian missions in the 19th and 20th centuries. In the latter half of the 20th century, many countries achieved independence and re-evaluated their relationship with the Christian faith. Surprisingly few Christians in these countries rejected the Christianity that had sometimes appeared to play a role in suppressing them.

Part of the reason for Christianity's continuing strength in many places has been the creation of indigenous expressions of the faith. Local clergy

Members of an African Pentecostal Church outside their building, with its Gothic-style doorway and corrugated-iron walls.

have been trained and given total responsibility for running national churches. New Christian symbols and liturgies have been developed so that worship comes out of the religious and cultural background of the people. However, in many places, this has resulted in an increased number of Churches, as less orthodox ways of expressing Christianity have sprung up.

Before Christ sent the Church into the world he sent the Spirit into the Church. The same order must be observed today.

JOHN STOTT,
BRITISH THEOLOGIAN

CHRISTIANITY WORLDWIDE

Contents

Expansion of Christianity

'Therefore go and make disciples of all nations.' Jesus' final words to his followers offered a huge missionary challenge, a challenge the Church has accepted to the extent that Christianity is now numerically the largest religion in the world.

After Jesus' death, resurrection and ascension, his apostles travelled extensively, making new disciples and teaching the new faith. The early churches, established around the Mediterranean, were attacked by the Roman authorities because they refused to recognize Roman emperors as gods or to worship the Roman gods. Many Christians were killed for their beliefs.

By 60 CE Christianity had reached many parts of the Roman empire, and around 300 CE Armenia became the first officially Christian nation. Outside the Roman empire, the new religion was a large minority in the Persian empire, especially from around 450 CE when the heretical Nestorian Church based on the teachings of Nestorius, patriarch of Constantinople, began there. The Nestorian Church spread to China and then into Afghanistan and India.

The Persians took control of Jerusalem in 615, with the Christian Byzantine empire reclaiming it soon afterwards. However, it was captured by the Arab Muslims in 637 and, apart from a short period between 1099 and 1187, during the Crusades, it has not been under direct Christian influence since.

Constantinople, the capital of the Byzantine empire, was conquered by the Turkish Muslims in 1453, an event which marked the end of the ancient Roman-Byzantine-Christian empire. The Mongols,

The Crusades were a series of largely unsuccessful attempts by an alliance of Western European nations to wrest control of the Holy Land from Muslim forces. The illustration by William of Tyre (c. 1130–85) shows Crusaders bombarding Nicea using human heads as ammunition in 1098.

St Ignatius Loyola (1491–1556), the founder of the Jesuit movement. The Jesuits were committed to spreading the Catholic faith, often in difficult and hostile situations. *Saint Ignatius of Loyola* by the French School (17th century).

> *This is the true sequence of mission: a surpassing awareness of the reality of Christ, corporately shared, expressing itself in thankfulness and wonder, causing the world to ask questions to which an answer must be given in a form that every hearer can understand.*
>
> JOHN V. TAYLOR,
> ENGLISH ANGLICAN BISHOP

especially under Tamerlane (c. 1336–1405), destroyed most of the Christian communities in Central Asia, and in China the communities simply withered and died.

Renewed advances

Things improved for missionary Christians in the 18th and 19th centuries. Key figures included William Carey (1761–1834) in India and James Hudson Taylor (1832–1905) in China. By the 18th century the Islamic Turks had stopped invading Europe, and a period of religious change and economic ferment in Europe led to its expansion into the Americas, Asia and Africa. The emigrants took Christianity with them and, by the time of the first International Missionary Conference in 1910, Christian missionaries had reached many areas of the world. Protestant missionary organizations were particularly strong in the early 20th century.

The Americas and Southern Africa became predominantly Christian; majority Christian countries were forming in much of Central Africa; and Christian majorities were also created in Australia and New Zealand. In the late 20th and early 21st centuries, many people have come to think that the countries most in need of evangelization now are the Western ones.

William Carey and his family land in India. His motto was 'Expect great things from God, and attempt great things for God.' He is regarded as the father of modern missions.

North America

In the USA far more people regularly attend worship than in any other traditionally Christian culture. Numerically, the strongest Churches are the Roman Catholic, Methodist and Baptist Churches.

By any standards North America is a very religious culture. Membership of Christian Churches in America has grown from about 15 per cent at the nation's beginning in 1783 to over 60 per cent today, while church attendance consistently hovers around 45 per cent of the population – compared with less than 10 per cent in Britain and other European countries. Surveys show that over 90 per cent of the American people identify themselves with some religious group or other.

America, like the Athens of St Paul's day, is very religious.
EDWIN GAUSTAD

Established Churches

In recent years growth rates for the established Christian denominations have levelled off and even begun to decline. The Roman Catholic Church remains the single largest denomination with about 25 per cent of the North American population claiming allegiance. In recent years, however, this Church has been under increasing pressure, with many members dissenting from its teaching on such issues as contraception, abortion and the death penalty. The Roman Catholic Church in America also suffers from a chronic lack of men offering themselves for the priesthood – a situation due more than anything else to the Church's insistence on clerical celibacy.

The Baptist Church, the largest Protestant denomination in the USA, has about 15 per cent of the population within its ranks. The various Methodist Churches take in 8 per cent of the population with Lutherans at around 5 per cent and Presbyterians at 3 per cent. Sizeable numbers also belong to the Disciples of Christ, the Episcopal Church and the United Church. It is little wonder, therefore, that G.K. Chesterton described America as 'the nation with the soul of a Church'.

New Churches

An important feature of American Church life has been the growth of smaller Christian groups during the 20th century. The Native American Church, which gains its membership from several Indian tribes, has 25,000 adherents, while the Plymouth Brethren, which started in England in the 19th century, has 100,000 members. The fundamentalist American Baptist Association claims to have over one million members. Various Holiness Churches, such as the Church of the Nazarene and the Free Methodist Church of North America, claim to have over 750,000 members. But the most phenomenal growth of all belongs to the major Pentecostal Churches: the Church of God in Christ has four million members, mostly black, the Assemblies of God has two million and the Church of God has two million.

Worshippers pack the vast Crystal Cathedral in Los Angeles.

Latin America

Two recent developments in Latin America have loosened the traditional hold that the Roman Catholic Church has had over the population: the growth of liberation theology and the proliferation of evangelical, largely Pentecostal, groups.

The pageantry of the Roman Catholic Church displayed in an Easter procession through the town of Cotacachi in Ecuador.

Until recently the people of Latin America have traditionally identified themselves with the Roman Catholic Church. Ninety per cent of the population professed to be Catholic, and more than half of the world's Roman Catholics were Latin American. However, two factors in recent years have weakened the control of the Church over its members in the 27 countries of Latin America.

Liberation theology

Since a conference of Latin American bishops in 1968 at Medellín, Colombia, the influence of liberation theology has spread throughout Latin America. Initially welcomed by the Roman Catholic Church, it was later viewed with deep suspicion due to the influence

> *The poor man, the other, reveals the totally Other to us.*
>
> GUSTAVO GUTTIÉREZ, LIBERATION THEOLOGIAN

The stark simplicity of an evangelical church in Lima, Peru.

Church building has been so rapid in Brazil that, at one time, new Evangelical Churches were opening at the rate of five a week in Rio de Janeiro.

of Marxism on some Latin American theologians and Church leaders. The basic argument of liberation theology is that the Church should be concerned with reflection, action (praxis) and raising the awareness of poor people about the need to act to secure social justice. Sin is not only the result of personal failings but also of social inequality, and Christians are obliged to fight against both – with force, if necessary. The Church should be firmly on the side of the poor, preaching that personal, spiritual and political salvation are different aspects of the same thing.

In Brazil and El Salvador, among other countries, small communities of 15 to 20 families, led by laypeople, have been formed to study the Bible and apply it to their own situations. In Brazil alone there were 100,000 such groups by 1985. These lessened the power of the Roman Catholic Church by encouraging members to study the Bible for themselves and develop their own strategies for improving their lives.

Evangelical groups

Just over 50 per cent of the population of Latin America now claim allegiance to the Roman Catholic Church. Since the mid 1970s evangelical Christianity has taken root in Latin America in a big way. Pentecostal Churches now account for 75 per cent of its 18 million Protestants. Although some of this growth has been prompted by evangelization from outside (largely North American), much of it has been indigenous.

Africa

Since the 1960s, the progress of the Christian gospel in Africa has been spectacular. All of the major denominations, plus thousands of much smaller independent Churches, have greatly increased their membership.

By the year 1990 about 50 per cent of all Africans were Church members, while 42 per cent were Muslim. Only sub-Saharan Africa has been left largely untouched. Thousands have been converted to Christianity in countries such as Mali and Ethiopia, while the populations of countries such as Kenya, Congo and Lesotho are more than 70 per cent Christian.

The African Church

Much of the rapid expansion of the Christian Church in Africa has been due to the work of

The Coptic Church is a very early branch of Christianity, and is confined mostly to North-Eastern Africa. A Coptic service in progress in Sudan.

missionaries from overseas. The number working in Africa increased from about 12,000 in 1925 to over 45,000 by 1980, and the Roman Catholic Church has been particularly effective in this. In 1960 there were an estimated 27 million Catholics in Africa, but this figure is likely

Children praying in their Sunday school in Mozambique.

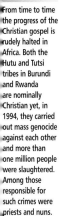

This tiny building in Kenya is typical of those used by the thousands of indigenous Churches which have sprung up all over Africa.

From time to time the progress of the Christian gospel is rudely halted in Africa. Both the Hutu and Tutsi tribes in Burundi and Rwanda are nominally Christian yet, in 1994, they carried out mass genocide against each other and more than one million people were slaughtered. Among those responsible for such crimes were priests and nuns.

INDEPENDENT CHURCHES

The last two decades of the 20th century saw a very rapid growth in the number of indigenous Churches in the world – Churches with one linguistic group living in a particular area. Seventy per cent of all indigenous Churches are to be found in Africa. By the year 2000 there were over 600 such Churches in Africa, with a total membership of over 30 million people. The theology of many of these Churches, however, is only loosely Christian.

to reach 120 million by 2010, meaning that over 10 per cent of the world's Roman Catholics will live on the continent of Africa. In many countries, however, the local Catholic Church has declared itself independent from the Pope, with important decisions being taken by indigenous Church leaders.

By 2010 there will be an estimated 25 million Anglicans (up from 3 million in 1960) and 33 million Orthodox believers (up from 14 million in 1960).

To cope with this dramatic

increase in numbers the various Churches have had to change their attitudes quickly. The need has been for a rapid Africanization of the clergy, with senior positions being occupied by national rather than foreign leaders. The Roman Catholic Church has found this the most difficult, but there have been rapid changes since 1960 even so. The consequences for the worldwide Church have been huge, with African clergy now able to exert a considerable influence. This was very noticeable at the 1998 Lambeth Conference of the Anglican Church. The Roman Catholic Church has also had to take a long, hard look at its teachings on issues such as marriage, divorce, family life and the role of women, since its traditional teaching has often conflicted with African culture.

> *To represent Jesus Christ as the first-born among many brethren who with him together form the Church is in true keeping with African notions.*
>
> HARRY SAWYERR, PROTESTANT THEOLOGIAN FROM SIERRA LEONE

Asia and Australasia

The continent of Asia, with 50 per cent of the world's population, should offer great opportunities for the Christian gospel, but it has always been a very difficult mission field. There are, however, many encouraging signs.

Although only about 3.5 per cent of the Asian population are Christians, this still means that 10 per cent of all Christians are Asian.

China

To control Christianity in China the Chinese government has created two state Churches: the Catholic Patriotic Association and the Three-Self Patriotic Movement. Many churches have been allowed to reopen in China since 1979, after the Cultural Revolution. In 1980 theological colleges were allowed to receive students and the printing of Bibles and other Christian literature was authorized. Since the Tiananmen Square massacre in 1989, however, the government has clamped down on house churches and arrested many of their pastors. There are thought to be between 30 to 70 million Christians in China.

India and Pakistan

There are over 7,000 foreign

Much of the growth of the Church takes place through small groups. A Tagalog family in Manila read the Bible together.

AUSTRALIA

Around 70 per cent of Australians identify with a Christian denomination. However, only about 10 per cent of the population attend a weekly service and this figure appears to be declining slowly. About half of all church attenders are Roman Catholic – there has been a strong Catholic presence in Australia since the arrival of the Irish convicts in the very early days of the colony, and later immigrant communities from countries such as Italy have complemented this influence.

In recent years the Pentecostal denominations have grown rapidly, and over 10 per cent of attenders on any Sunday will be to these churches.

> *God seems especially patient in Asia. Space is vast. History is long. Culture is rich. Persons are numerous. The heart nourished by such culture embraces deep emotions. The soul formed in such history is very patient. And the mind grown out of such vast space has plenty of room.*
>
> CHOAN-SENG SONG,
> TAIWANESE THEOLOGIAN

The largest Christian community in the world – Paul Cho's Full Gospel Central Church in Seoul – claims to have a membership in excess of 600,000.

missionaries in India, although some have had restrictions placed on their activities in recent decades. One in every 50 Indians is thought to be Christian, whereas in Pakistan, where Christians sometimes feel threatened by the Muslim government, it is slightly less.

South-East Asia

Christians make up 8 per cent of the Vietnamese population – about four million people – and 90 per cent of these belong to the Roman Catholic Church.

The Evangelical Church has also prospered, securing over 400,000 members.

Little is known about the Church in North Korea, but in South Korea the Christian community numbers over 13 million – more than 30 per cent of the overall population. Further growth of the Church in South Korea, however, is hampered by the fact that it is split into over 100 sects and denominations.

Indonesia is the home of the largest Muslim community in the world, but even here the Church has been successful. Some 12 per cent of the population belong to a Christian Church – 15 million people in all – and 25 per cent of these are Roman Catholic.

In recent years large numbers of South Koreans have embraced the Christian faith; the Full Gospel Church in Seoul is the world's largest church.

Europe

Although there are encouraging signs of Church growth in many parts of the world, the same cannot be said of Western Europe, where church attendance and allegiance have declined dramatically since the middle of the 20th century.

Since the end of the Second World War, Church membership and attendance in Western Europe have decreased rapidly. Less than 10 per cent of Europe's population now attend church regularly, and there are clear signs that people have not only rejected the religious teachings of the Church, but are also refusing to accept its guidance in matters of personal and social morality.

Western Europe

Surveys carried out in France in the last decade of the 20th century revealed that 80 per cent of the population identified themselves with the Roman Catholic Church, although just 10 per cent regularly attended Mass.

Official figures in Germany maintain that 90 per cent of the population are Christians – 29 million Protestant and 27 million Roman Catholic, with evangelicals being estimated at eight million. Most Protestants belong to one of 17 Lutheran or Reformed territorial national Churches.

Ninety per cent of the populations of Belgium and Luxembourg are baptized members of the Roman Catholic Church, but church attendance in both countries has declined markedly in the last two decades.

According to a 1989 census in the Netherlands, 36 per cent claimed to belong to the Roman Catholic Church, 28 per cent said they were Protestant (mainly belonging to the Dutch Reformed Church), 4 per cent were from other religious groups and 32 per cent had no religious allegiance. The leadership of the Roman Catholic Church in the Netherlands has been foremost among those demanding that the Church changes its stance on such issues as contraception and clerical celibacy.

Eastern Europe

Since the Iron Curtain was lifted at the beginning of the 1990s, the Christian Church has

Since 1920 the Czechoslovakian Catholic Church has been totally independent of the authorities in Rome – having abandoned clerical celibacy and encouraged lay participation in church government. Bishops are elected but not consecrated and the idea of apostolic succession is rejected. Many traditional Catholic doctrines such as original sin, purgatory and the veneration of saints are rejected.

prospered in Eastern Europe. There have, however, been many problems. Restrictions on the printing and dissemination of Bibles and Christian literature in Russia were lifted in 1990 and this has led to fierce interdenominational hostility. Many Protestant organizations have moved in from the West to compete for new converts, while the Roman Catholic Church has upset many by setting up parallel dioceses. The Baptist Church remains the most successful Protestant Church in Russia. However, the traditional guardian of Christianity in the country, the Orthodox Church, has opposed the freedom given to new religious groups and sought to encourage the

Christian mission to Europe and North America is a matter of urgent necessity because it is these countries that do the most harm to humanity and nature as a whole; exercise more power for good or evil; call themselves Christian and hence are more damaging to the witness of the gospel; and are more dehumanized, more alienated from the values of the kingdom, and more difficult to convert.

TISSA BALASURIYA,
SRI LANKAN THEOLOGIAN

Poland enjoyed greater freedom than anywhere else in Eastern Europe. Polish Catholics were active in the Solidarity Movement that led to the downfall of Communism in 1989, but the Church leaders have shown themselves to be very conservative and this has hindered further progress.

The lifting of restrictions on Christian activity in Russia and Eastern Europe has not been without its problems. The Orthodox Church, which in some countries had benefited from cooperation with Communist authorities, found itself open to competition. A small Orthodox church in Romania.

government to authorize no other expression of Christianity than its own.

With the election of a Polish Pope in 1978 the Church in

Spirituality embraces every aspect of life, both individual and corporate. The Hebrew tradition stresses spirituality as integration; the Greek tradition, on the other hand, puts its emphasis on desire – an insistent longing to experience God in this world as well as in the next. In Christian spirituality the two aspects of integration and desire are combined, and this has lent Christianity astonishing vitality and inventiveness.

Christians have developed a wide variety of spiritual disciplines, including prayer and meditation, worship, pilgrimage and personal Bible reading. For Christians their interior

A portable hand-carved and painted icon from Ethiopia representing scenes from the life of Christ.

spiritual life affects everything they do, however insignificant. Clear expressions of the outworking of the Holy Spirit in their lives can be seen in areas of social welfare and ethics, as well as in art, music, literature and architecture.

> *Spirituality is a way of living; it is also a way of following Jesus.*
>
> CONSUELO DEL PRADO,
> PERUVIAN CATHOLIC SISTER

SPIRITUALITY

Contents

Discipleship

During fewer than three years of public ministry, Jesus told people about the proximity of God's kingdom, calling those who listened and responded to his message to a life of service and discipleship.

People who followed religious teachers at the time of Jesus attached themselves to those whose teachings attracted them most. However, Jesus turned this around when choosing his own closest disciples by calling *them* to follow *him*. Jesus also extended a general call to discipleship to others, which they were free to accept or refuse. Becoming a disciple involved a radical change of heart, a total commitment to Jesus which the Gospel-writers often characterized as a willingness to leave everything and everyone else behind.

The story of the rich young ruler illustrates this perfectly. To this young man, who claimed to

If anyone would come after me, he must deny himself and take up his cross and follow me. For whoever wants to save his life will lose it, but whoever loses his life for me and for the gospel will save it.

MARK 8:34–35

Christ demonstrated the need for his disciples to have the attitude of servants. *Jesus Washing Peter's Feet* (1876) by Ford Madox Brown (1821–93).

have kept all the Jewish commandments from his youth, Jesus said, 'One thing you lack. Go, sell everything you have and give to the poor, and you will have treasure in heaven. Then come, follow me.' In the Gospels those who followed

My command is this: love each other as I have loved you. Greater love has no one than this, that one lay down one's life for one's friends.

JOHN 15:12–13

Jesus 'left everything' including work, family and children. For some, being a disciple even included celibacy, which they embraced for the sake of God and his kingdom.

Spiritual disciplines

The outworking of Christian spirituality through prayer, pilgrimage or worship enables people to draw closer to God and makes Christian discipleship more meaningful. No two Christians are the same so no two paths towards Christian maturity are identical either. Within Christianity different people may follow distinct paths to God through Jesus, using different styles of prayer, worship or music to help them in their walks of faith.

91

The Sermon on the Mount

The Sermon on the Mount brings together the teaching of Jesus on a whole range of themes. Nowhere else in the Gospels is the radical nature of Christian discipleship spelled out more clearly.

Christian discipleship in the Gospels means making a personal, and often very costly, decision to follow Jesus that will affect every dimension of life. It changes relationships, shapes personal attitudes to property and wealth, gives a new order of priorities and lends fresh meaning to love. It brings a whole new perspective to personal fulfilment.

Christian discipleship
Frequently in talking about Christian discipleship Jesus would take a saying from the Jewish Law (the Torah) and deepen it with his own interpretation. So Jesus widens the teaching of the Ten Commandments on murder to outlaw the showing of destructive anger; he alters the law that allowed retaliation in certain circumstances to rule out any acts of vengeance; and he broadens the command to love one's neighbours to include loving one's enemies.

In one simple command-ment, often called the Golden

> *In everything, do to others what you would have them do to you, for this sums up the Law and the Prophets.*
>
> THE GOLDEN RULE, MATTHEW 7:12

Rule, Jesus summed up the new Christian law of love. He told his followers they should treat others in exactly the same way as they would like to be treated themselves.

Changing behaviour
Jesus made it clear that genuine Christian discipleship must also affect moral and ethical behaviour. He gives two examples in the Sermon on the Mount:

◆ Adultery – the Ten Commandments outlaw adultery, but Jesus went beyond this simple statement to the heart of the matter: to be true to his teaching a person must not just avoid committing adultery, they must not even want to in the first place. Entering the kingdom of God

The Sermon on the Mount is full of radical insights and teaching that turned the ideas and attitudes of the time upside down. Christ's teaching on adultery is one such example. *The Woman Taken in Adultery* by Rembrandt van Rijn (1606–69).

is such a serious matter that no sacrifice is too great to make it possible.

◆ Divorce – Jesus seems to allow divorce on the grounds of adultery, although in other circumstances he clearly rules it out. What is clear is that adulterous relationships and/or divorce should have no place in the Christian life.

Prayer

Prayer is primarily about a relationship with God and is fundamental to the life of a Christian. Prayer is possible because the way to God has been opened up by Christ. In Christ, God can be known, loved and adored.

Although prayer plays a very important part in public worship, it is private prayer that is central to Christian spirituality. This is in keeping with Jesus' teaching in the Sermon on the Mount, in which he tells his followers to 'go into your room, close the door and pray to your Father, who is unseen'.

There are traditionally three key elements in prayer:

◆ thanksgiving, because in Christ God has reconciled humanity to himself.
◆ penitence, because in Christ God has forgiven and continues to forgive humankind.
◆ intercession (praying for others), because in Christ God has declared a purpose for humanity. Jesus himself encourages his disciples to make requests for others known to the Father.

Many Christians set aside time each day to spend in personal prayer and this is often accompanied by Bible reading and reflection.

Orthodox Christians often use an icon to help them pray. An icon is a stylized painting of Jesus, his mother Mary or the saints. Icons are not realistic as such, because they are simply representations of the divine world, so are often called 'windows to the eternal'.

Roman Catholics sometimes use a rosary (a string of beads) to help them meditate on key events in the life of Jesus. Evangelicals and charismatics are often comfortable expressing their thoughts and feelings directly to God without any prayer aids.

Three specific prayers are widely used by many Christians:

The name 'rosary' for this string of beads comes from the Latin *rosarium*, meaning 'rose garden' or 'garland'. Roman Catholics use the rosary as an aid to meditation.

Surveys suggest that fewer than 1⬤ per cent of people pray regularly, but over 90 per cent have been known to pray when frightened or in great need.

Hail Mary, full of grace, the Lord is with thee. Blessed art thou among women, and blessed is the fruit of thy womb, Jesus. Holy Mary, Mother of God, pray for us sinners, now, and at the hour of our death. Amen.

THE HAIL MARY

◆ the Lord's Prayer or Our Father, which is recorded in the Sermon on the Mount and which Jesus taught his disciples to use.

◆ the Hail Mary or Ave Maria, a hymn of praise to the Virgin Mary used by Roman Catholics. The Catholic Church regularly offers prayers to Mary, seeking her help and intercession with God.

The act of praying together gives Christians the opportunity to remember the needs of others – and support them.

MEDITATION

Meditation is a spiritual activity which is found in many religions and some Christians use it as part of their prayer life. Meditation is a mixture of silent and vocal prayer. Some people read a passage from the Bible, particularly from the Gospels, and try to imagine themselves in the scene; this helps them to experience scripture more deeply and to use their emotions as well as their minds. This form of prayer was particularly advocated by St Ignatius Loyola (1491–1556) and is widely used today by Christians of all traditions.

◆ the Jesus Prayer consists of the constant repetition of a short sentence, 'Lord Jesus Christ, Son of God, have mercy on me, a sinner,' and is associated with the Orthodox tradition.

Monasticism

The Christian monastic tradition goes back to the early centuries of the faith, but it was not until the sixth century that a common way of monastic life was formed. The tradition has made an enormous spiritual contribution to the Christian Church.

Isolation from the world in a spiritual sense is reflected in the physical remoteness of the monastery of St Nicholas Anapafsas in Greece.

Some of the early Christians wanted to dedicate themselves totally to God so, following the example of Jesus in the wilderness, they travelled to the desert to live lives of austerity and prayer. To begin with they lived as hermits, but soon formed communities known as monasteries. Some of the earliest monasteries were built on Mount Athos in Greece, where more than 20 monastic communities remain today.

The Rule

St Benedict (c. 480–c. 550) laid down the Rule by which all monasteries and convents have

Christianity is not primarily a theological system, an ethical system, a ritual system, a social system or an ecclesiastical system – it is a person: it's Jesus Christ, and to be a Christian is to know him and to follow him and believe in him.

JOHN STOTT, BRITISH THEOLOGIAN

The oldest extant copy of the Rule of St Benedict (English, c. 700) The passage shown describes observances in winter.

APOSTOLIC AND CONTEMPLATIVE ORDERS

Most of today's religious orders are apostolic, meaning that they work outside the community in various caring professions such as nursing and teaching. They return to the community at the end of the day to further their spiritual vocation of prayer. Some religious orders, however, exist to develop a contemplative way of life, with the emphasis on withdrawal into an enclosed world which has little contact with anyone outside the community. Contemplative orders place a high degree of importance on silence within the community. While some time is given over to work and recreation, the focus is heavily on prayer, reading and studying.

organized their spiritual and communal life ever since. The Rule stipulates that all monks and nuns should live:

◆ a life of poverty. Jesus told a rich young man to go and sell everything he had if he wanted to be a disciple. Similarly, those entering a religious order must use their wealth and goods for the benefit of the whole community. One reason for this is that most religious orders work among the poor and needy and it would be inappropriate for them not to share the same way of life.

◆ a life of chastity. Members of a religious order should not form strong emotional attachments with others since they are, in a real sense, married to God. Marriage would divert them from their main task of working for the kingdom of God.

◆ a life of obedience. Those who enter a monastery or a convent are expected to live in total obedience to the will of God, as expressed by the leader of the community. Leaders are chosen by the monks or nuns themselves for the exceptional holiness of their lives.

Modern technology can benefit even members of an order that goes back for centuries.

Saints, Heroes and Martyrs

Both the Orthodox and the Roman Catholic Churches honour certain people as saints after their deaths, while in Protestant Churches martyrs and others are looked up to as examples of faith, although they are not given any formal status.

The word 'saint' refers to someone who is holy, set apart for the service of God, an example to all of great faith. The word can be used in two ways:

◆ The phrase the 'communion of saints' recognizes that the whole Church, the body of believers, is made up of saints.

◆ The saints are those who have passed through a process of canonization by the Church which officially recognizes them for the holiness of their lives. It is in this sense that the Roman Catholic and Orthodox Churches set apart special festival days on which the contribution made by these people to the Church can be celebrated.

In the Orthodox Church, many saints are represented by icons, in which they have not only halos of light around their heads to symbolize sainthood, but also light shining from their faces to show they are special witnesses to God. Many Christians believe they can ask the saints in heaven to pray for them. The Virgin Mary, as the Mother of Jesus, is thought to be supreme over all saints because she was chosen to bear Jesus, the Son of God and Redeemer of the world.

> *The Lord is wonderful in his saints.*
>
> EASTERN ORTHODOX SAYING

Heroes and martyrs

The original martyrs were the apostles, witnesses of the life and resurrection of Jesus, but as the Church passed through many periods of persecution, 'martyrs' came to refer to those had lost their lives for their faith. Since the end of the second century CE the anniversary of a martyr's death (*natalis* – his or her heavenly birthday) has been kept as a day of liturgical celebration. Soon martyrs were venerated as powerful intercessors in heaven, their relics were highly prized and numerous legends were attached to them.

During the 20th century many people have been highly admired for their courage and commitment. Some have lost their lives for their faith, such as Maximilian Kolbe (1894–1941), a Catholic priest who met death at the hands of the Nazis through volunteering to replace a young man sentenced to death by starvation, and Dietrich Bonhoeffer (1905–45), a Lutheran pastor who was hanged by the Gestapo in the last few weeks of the Second World War for his part in a plot to execute Hitler.

Others, though, have won universal respect and recognition because of the work they have done. Mother Teresa of Calcutta (1910–1997), founder of the Missionaries of Charity, went to Calcutta in 1948 to teach the children of the poor and to care for the destitute and helpless. The work of the organization she founded has become legendary for its selfless love and devotion to the poor.

Adoring Saints (detail from panel) by Jacopo di Cione, (active c. 1362, died 1398/1400).

Pilgrimage

A pilgrimage is a journey to a holy place undertaken as an act of religious devotion, to pay penance or to offer thanks for the answering of a prayer.

Although pilgrimage plays a central role in many religions, it has been less important in Christianity. However, millions of pilgrims over the years have undertaken journeys to special holy sites and they continue to do so today.

Why go on a pilgrimage?

In the main it has been Catholics who have undertaken pilgrimages over the centuries. Pilgrims have undertaken such journeys because they want:

◆ to receive God's forgiveness for sins they have committed. During the Middle Ages, for instance, Canterbury became a popular destination because pilgrims were told that if they went there their sins would be wiped out and they would create merit in purgatory for friends and relatives.
◆ to thank God for a blessing they have received, or to receive

Santiago de Compostela in Spain, reputed to house the bones of St James.

physical healing. Over two million pilgrims descend on Lourdes in France each year because the waters are believed to have special healing properties.
◆ to visit the places that are significant to their faith. Thousands travel to the Holy Land each year, especially during the festivals of Christmas and Easter, so that they can visit Bethlehem, Jerusalem and other places mentioned in the Gospels. Other places associated with a vision of the Virgin Mary, such as Walsingham in England, Lourdes in France, Knock in Ireland and Fatima in Portugal, are all visited in large numbers by Catholic pilgrims. Santiago de Compostela in Spain has been a pilgrimage destination since the ninth century because it is believed that the bones of St James, a disciple of Jesus, are buried there. The Catholic

Christian pilgrimage started in the fourth century when Helena, mother of the Christian Roman emperor, Constantine, discovered the remains of three crosses in Jerusalem. No one was sure which was part of the cross on which Jesus had died, so, legend has it, each one of them was laid on the body of a sick woman until they found the one that cured her – the true cross of Christ. From this time onwards relics became a key part of Catholic worship.

> *Of what avail is it to go across the sea to Christ if all the time I lose the Christ that is within me here.*
>
> LEO TOLSTOY (1828–1910),
> RUSSIAN NOVELIST

Church has always valued relics highly. Relics are the physical remains of a holy person and are often incorporated into the altar of a church.

The question of whether people are actually cured at these holy places of pilgrimage remains unanswered. Perhaps the main purposes of pilgrimage are spiritual growth and warm fellowship with other pilgrims along the route. For some Christians pilgrimage is a valuable part of their spiritual journey.

Pilgrims journeying on foot, horseback or by boat from the Flemish *The Travels of Sir John Mandeville*, 15th century.

Art

The Christian Church was the earliest patron of art and so, unsurprisingly, art and worship have always been closely linked while Christian themes have inspired many of the world's outstanding painters.

From the time that the early Christians spent in the catacombs under Rome, trying to escape from bitter persecution, art and Christian worship have been intertwined. The numerous wall-paintings that survive from this period show Christ represented as a fish or a young shepherd, the Church symbolized by a ship, immortality represented by a peacock and hope depicted as an anchor. This is the earliest Christian art.

From Saxon times onwards stone carvings showing scenes from the Bible or from the lives of various saints were used to decorate churches. Many of these have survived, although work from the same period in wood, as well as embroidery, vestments and altar frontals, has long since disappeared.

Art and faith

Because the Christian Church was the only major patron of the arts for centuries, religious themes dominated art throughout the medieval and Renaissance periods. To begin with, artists were reluctant to portray the agony of Christ at his crucifixion, but once this had passed the passion of Christ became an artistic preoccupation. A strong appeal was made to the onlooker's emotions as Jesus' judgment

Wall-painting from the catacomb of St Priscilla showing the Madonna and child with a prophet.

under Pilate, whipping by the soldiers, nakedness, humiliation and suffering were vividly portrayed. There is a clear link between Grünewald's *The Crucifixion*, painted in the early 16th century, and Salvador Dalí's *Christ of St John of the Cross* (1951), a stark painting of Christ dying for the world.

A stained-glass window designed for a Roman Catholic Cathedral depicting some modern saints.

Artists have often attempted to portray Christ in the clothes of their time to contemporize him. Stanley Spencer, an English artist, painted Christ carrying his cross through the village of Cookham in 1920, using portraits of people who lived there as part of the crowd.

> *We need our artists to remind us not only of who we are but also of what the world is.*
>
> VERONICA BRADY,
> AUSTRALIAN WRITER

matter, so are unique in religious art.

Stained-glass windows

Many church buildings are ornamented with stained-glass windows. In the Middle Ages glass was regarded as magical and even divine. Glass-makers could turn the lowest of elements, earth, into a durable and 'sun-comprehending' substance. It was its ability to transmit light that made glass so special. In religious terms, light symbolized the quality of the Holy Spirit, so glass was ideally suited to the interpretation of spiritual themes. Stained-glass windows were also an extremely valuable visual teaching aid at a time when the vast majority of the population was illiterate.

Icons

In the East, religious expression through art has survived in the unique form of icons – highly stylized painting on wood of the holy family, the Virgin Mary or the saints. Such paintings are created in prayer, so can act as stimuli to spiritual devotion. Icons are extensions of their subject

Music

Music has always played a part in Christian worship, from the psalms, through plainsong, hymns and sacred music, to the modern music of Taizé and other forms.

The collection of 150 psalms in the Old Testament were sung both in the Jewish Temple and in the later synagogues and they were also used by the early Christians in their worship. These psalms are still used widely in Christian worship today, as well as being adapted for use as Gregorian plainsong and Taizé chant. In the Benedictine monastic tradition, the rotation of different psalms is a key element in daily worship.

A new song

The psalms sang the praises of God the Creator for the beauties of the earth, but had nothing to say about the specific Christian revelation of the life, death and resurrection of Jesus. From the early years of Christianity comes the Latin *Te Deum Laudamus*: 'We praise thee, O God, we acknowledge thee to be the Lord... Thou art the King of glory, O Christ,' and this is still used in worship. New versions of the psalms were published in the 16th and 17th centuries before the first of many hymns in English was written by Isaac Watts (1674–1748). His most well-known contribution is 'When I Survey the Wondrous Cross'.

The range of hymns was greatly widened by the contributions of Charles Wesley (1707–88) who wrote over 6,000 hymns, many of which are still widely used today. Around the same time John Newton (1725–1804), a converted slave-trader, and Philip Doddridge (1702–51), an Anglican, were producing many hymns for use in worship.

The choir plays a leading part in many traditional church services.

AFRICAN-AMERICAN SPIRITUALS

The black slaves in America developed their own musical form, mixing African rhythms with Christian themes. The 'spirituals'

that resulted are deeply moving expressions of joy and hope in the midst of darkness and suffering. According to James Cone in *The Spirituals and the Blues*:

The basic idea of the spirituals is that slavery contradicts God; it is a denial of his will. To be enslaved is to be declared nobody, and that form of existence contradicts God's creation of people to be his children.

Moving words and expressive music in an African Baptist Church in Savannah, Georgia.

Sacred music

There was a great flowering of sacred music, especially the oratorio, from 1600 onwards. J.S. Bach is considered, by common consent, to be the greatest religious composer of all. An orthodox Lutheran, Bach wrote over 200 church cantatas together with two great settings of the *Passion* – according to John (1724) and according to Matthew (1727). Around the same time G.F. Handel wrote the *Messiah* (1741). Josef Haydn's *The Creation* (1798) was a devoutly devotional paean of praise to the Almighty God. Many of today's leading composers – such as James MacMillan, a Scottish Presbyterian, and John

Tavener, a Greek Orthodox – continue to find inspiration in the scriptures and the liturgy of the Church.

Contemporary music

Both the Taizé community in France and the Iona community in Scotland have produced music that has found a worldwide audience. Today, many churches have swapped choir and organ for worship bands who play guitar-led music written by worship leaders such as Matt Redman, Graham Kendrick, Andy Piercy and Dave Clifton.

Literature

In countries where Christianity has been a dominant cultural and social influence, it has inspired much great literature. This has been particularly true in the Western world where, up until the 17th and 18th centuries, the Christian view of the universe was generally accepted; however, since the Enlightenment, people have sought to begin anew and to shape human communication and culture on the assumption that humankind is autonomous.

In the first few centuries of Christianity, much Christian writing took the form of grammar or theology. Augustine of Hippo (354–430) profoundly influenced future writers with his emphasis on truth and moral instruction above considerations of style. Despite this, Western writing flourished and many significant writers of both prose and poetry appeared, reaching their peak in the 13th century with the Italian poet, Dante Alighieri (1265–1321). Dante wrote one of the masterpieces of world literature: the *Divine Comedy*, a long dramatic poem that reflects the highest culture of the period and takes as its subject the afterlife, as experienced in hell, purgatory and heaven. The *Divine Comedy* is a Christian allegory about the soul's vision of sin, its cleansing from guilt and its rising to new life. All writers before the Reformation were officially Christian. Works

A group of Dominican friars present a book to Augustine from the *Legendary of Dominican Nuns of Holy Cross* (German, after 1271), Regensburg.

such as Geoffrey Chaucer's poetry were full of Christian assumptions, both implicit and explicit.

> *Just as good literature and good art raise and ennoble character, so bad literature and bad art degrade it.*
>
> DONALD COGGAN, FORMER ARCHBISHOP OF CANTERBURY

A new direction

The 15th and 16th centuries are often regarded as the time when the Western mind broke free of Christian dogma and began to assert its freedom. However, consciously non-Christian writing did not appear until well into the 18th century. Even though great writers such as Shakespeare, Rabelais and Cervantes did not write specifically Christian drama and fiction, they wrote against the moral backdrop of the generally accepted Christian view of the universe. In recent centuries, as Christian belief has declined in the West and the accepted worldview has changed and fragmented, so the Christian contribution to the world of literature is increasingly difficult to identify. Writers who have managed to convey their Christian vision through their work stand out as exceptions and include people such as Leo Tolstoy, Fyodor Dostoevsky, T.S. Eliot and C.S. Lewis.

FYODOR DOSTOEVSKY

Born in Moscow in 1821, the son of a doctor, Dostoevsky suffered much during his life, including a 10-year sentence in Siberia for belonging to an underground movement; he was also a chronic gambler and endured epileptic seizures. In 1866 he published *Crime and Punishment*, a deeply spiritual novel and one which won him much praise. He spent much time wandering about Europe – in Germany, Switzerland and Italy – often in desperate poverty because of his gambling addiction. Books such as *The Idiot* (1868) and *The Possessed* (1871) added to his reputation as one of the finest of novelists, and in 1880 *The Brothers Karamazov* appeared, considered to be his greatest work. Dostoevsky's books are novels of ideas, full of brilliant characterizations and dramatic situations, and struggles between good and evil. His Russian Orthodox faith is particularly evident in *Crime and Punishment* and *The Brothers Karamazov*, where the characters search for redemption through suffering and love.

Architecture

For centuries people have built cathedrals, churches and chapels in which to worship God, and to express their deepest feelings about God and the spiritual life.

Architecture, like all art forms, has been highly susceptible to prevailing fashions over the centuries and that includes church buildings.

Churches and God

Church buildings over the years have passed through many styles. Among the influences have been:

◆ the Gothic style of architecture born in Northern France in the 12th century. Gothic buildings seem to soar up to heaven and they are filled with light and space, with a delicate stone framework. As European society generally experienced a great increase in wealth in the succeeding four centuries, so much of it was used to build new cathedrals and churches. Over 500 cathedrals alone were built between 1100 and 1500. Gothic churches express great confidence in the omnipotence and unchangeability of God. Workers used their skills freely to the glory of God.

The buttresses of Milan Cathedral, the last great cathedral to be built in the Gothic style of architecture that dominated Western Europe during the late middle ages. Its construction was based on a complex geometrical grid of intersecting circles and equilateral triangles.

◆ the Reformation. This 16th-century movement saw a strong reaction against the use of visual material in places of worship, together with a move away from worship based on the sacraments to one in which the Bible, the word of God, was paramount. Little money was available and simplicity was the key, with the pulpit rather than the altar being the focal point of the building.

◆ the Baroque style of architecture – a grand and ornate form which prevailed in Italy during the 17th and 18th

A church building often began with high hopes in the Gothic period, only for the money to run out before the construction was finished. Cologne Cathedral, for instance, took over 700 years to complete.

Modern materials and technology are used to great effect in the construction of the spectacular cathedral at Brasilia.

centuries and spread throughout mainland Europe, especially France and Spain. Baroque churches were built on a grand scale, with the immensity of the building designed to lead the worshipper into an experience of the grandeur of God.

In the 19th century, builders recognized that their church was not going to be a focal point but simply one of several religious buildings in their town or village. So they contructed essentially simple buildings and made little use of architecture to express

A Nonconformist chapel typical of the many thousands dotted throughout the towns and villages of Britain.

religious beliefs or spiritual aspirations.

In the 20th century, new materials became available and many church buildings became streamlined and functional, often fulfilling an ecumenical function. Materials such as concrete and plate glass were frequently used to produce light-filled churches in which excellent acoustics combined with stark architecture.

Roman Catholic and Eastern Orthodox Churches place much emphasis on sacraments and the liturgical year. For other Christians these are less important, and only Christmas and Easter are universally celebrated. However, all Christians share a commitment to meeting together regularly to worship God.

A sacrament can be defined as 'an outward and visible sign of an inward and spiritual grace'. The Roman Catholic and Eastern Orthodox Churches teach that there are seven sacraments:

◆ Communion
◆ baptism
◆ confirmation
◆ penance
◆ holy orders
◆ the anointing of the sick
◆ marriage.

A Easter procession in Guatemala includes this dramatic portrayal of the suffering of Christ.

All Churches base their worship around the Christian year, although Protestants tend to focus on just Christmas and Easter. The Christian year falls into three cycles: Christmas, Easter and Pentecost.

> *The whole world ought to be regarded as the visible part of a universal and continuing sacrament, and all man's activities as a sacramental, divine communion.*
>
> DUMITRU STANILOAE,
> ROMANIAN ORTHODOX THEOLOGIAN

SACRAMENTS, SERVICES AND THE CHRISTIAN YEAR

Contents

Mass and Holy Liturgy

The Mass is celebrated daily in every Roman Catholic Church as is the Holy Liturgy in Eastern Orthodox Churches.

At the outset of the Mass the priest invites the people to repent of their sins and seek God's forgiveness. Three Bible passages are then read before the priest preaches his homily, ending the first part of the Mass – the Liturgy of the Word. The service then moves on to the second part, the Liturgy of the Mass. Turning towards the altar the congregation recites the Nicene Creed affirming their faith in God the Father, Son and Holy Spirit, the Church and the life to come. The people bring forwards their gifts of bread, wine and money as the prayer of consecration is offered. It is at this point that Catholics believe the bread and wine become the actual body and blood of Jesus – a belief called transubstantiation. The people respond by saying, 'Christ has died, Christ is risen, Christ will come again,' summing up the Church's full belief in Jesus, its Saviour.

Penance

Traditionally, Catholics were encouraged to confess their sins privately to a priest before taking Communion. This is the sacrament of penance or reconciliation. After hearing the person's confession, the priest would pronounce forgiveness and bless the penitent, and perhaps suggest a penance to be performed. Orthodox Christians

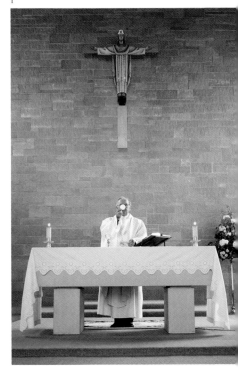

During the Mass the priest elevates the bread, or host. The word 'host' comes from the Latin *hostia*, meaning 'sacrificial victim'

THE BEAUTY OF THE LITURGY

The service of Holy Liturgy is usually complemented by an unaccompanied choir, which enhances the beauty of the liturgy. Orthodox Christians believe that they are taking part in an 'eternal liturgy', since eveything on earth is an image of an eternal pattern.

An Orthodox priest prepares the elements out of sight of the people.

the early Church the unbaptized were dismissed before the eucharist began and the remaining congregation was solemnly dismissed at the end. By the eighth century the term *missa* (dismissal) had been applied to the service as a whole.

have also traditionally been expected to spend time in contrition and fasting before receiving Communion.

The Holy Liturgy

Orthodox Christians believe that their Holy Liturgy has unique power and significance because it can be traced back to the earliest days of Christian worship. The first part of the liturgy, the Liturgy of the Word, bears a strong similarity to the Anglican/Episcopalian and Catholic Communion services. The climax to this part of the service occurs when the priest passes through the royal doors of the iconostasis carrying the Book of the Gospels (a beautifully decorated copy of

the Gospels) high above his head, surrounded by attendants carrying candles. Having read a passage from the book he then returns to the high altar.

Most of the Liturgy of the Faithful that follows is conducted by the priest behind the iconostasis, which symbolizes the gulf that exists between God and humankind brought about by sin. This gulf is so great that only the priest, by virtue of his ordination by God as Jesus' representative, is allowed to enter God's presence, symbolized by the high altar.

Orthodox Christians believe God comes to them through the bread and wine of Communion. The Liturgy of the Faithful begins with the preparation of these elements, during which the priest stands at the high altar with the royal doors of the iconostasis closed to remind the congregation of the holiness of Jesus' death. After the priest has consecrated the bread and wine he brings them through the royal doors and the people kneel to receive them. The priest places a piece of bread dipped in wine at the back of each communicant's throat using a long, silver spoon.

Protestant Communion

In Reformed Churches the service of Communion is almost invariably one of remembrance, providing an opportunity for worshippers to meditate on the death of Jesus.

In Reformed Churches the Communion service is often called the Lord's Supper or the Breaking of Bread, both of which are taken directly from the Bible. It is apparent that the early Christians often came together to share an ordinary meal both as an act of worship and also as a way of feeding the hungry in the Christian community.

The Lord's Supper

The Lord's Supper usually begins with the confession of sins and a reading from the Bible. The passage chosen may describe the last meal that Jesus ate with his disciples or Paul's description of the inception of the meal. The minister spends some time explaining the meaning of the passage and a collection is often taken up for the poor and needy.

The bread and wine are then consecrated to God in a prayer as the minister recounts the words spoken by Jesus at the Last Supper. In Methodist Churches the people usually come to the front to kneel at the rail to receive the bread and wine, but in Baptist Churches the elements are taken to the

For the tradition which I handed on to you came to me from the Lord himself: that on the night of his arrest the Lord Jesus took bread, and after giving thanks to God broke it and said: 'This is my body, which is for you; do this in memory of me.' In the same way, he took the cup after supper, and said: 'This cup is the new covenant sealed by my blood. Whenever you drink it, do this in memory of me.'

1 CORINTHIANS 11:23–25

Although the term 'Lord's Supper' comes from the New Testament it became popular as a description for Communion after Nicholas Ridley, a Protestant martyr, published *Brief Declaration of the Lord's Supper* in 1554, while in prison.

people by the leaders of the Church. As people take the bread they eat it at once to symbolize their immediate response to Christ's calling. The wine in small individual glasses is held back until everyone has eaten the bread so that they can drink together as a sign of unity in Christ.

The significance of the Lord's Supper

Protestants do not believe that the bread and wine become the body and blood of Christ during the service. They are simply reminders of his sacrifice. The Catholic belief in transubstantiation was emphatically rejected during the Protestant Reformation and this remains a major difference between the sacramental and

non-sacramental Churches. For Protestants the bread and wine are emblematic of far deeper spiritual realities. As they are taken, and consumed, they act as stimuli to meditation and reflection on the death of Jesus. This is why the minister, before distributing the bread and wine, tells the congregation to feed on Jesus in their hearts by faith with thanksgiving.

In Baptist Churches, communicants usually receive the wine in individual glasses, rather than from a shared cup.

Often a single loaf of bread is broken in the sight of the congregation, a reminder that Christ's death unites believers. The Bible instructs each person as they come to take Communion to be sure they have no divisive attitudes which might damage that unity.

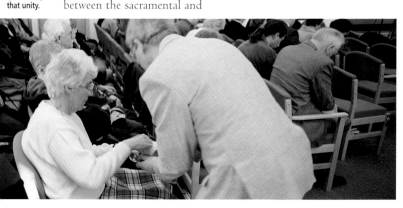

Worship Services

Some Protestant Churches do not celebrate Communion frequently and do not follow a liturgical pattern of prayer and worship. Instead, they create their own patterns of worship, with a heavy emphasis on song and hymn singing, Bible reading, intercessory prayer and preaching.

In some Protestant Churches, Communion is celebrated daily, but in the vast majority it is less frequent. The main way that Protestant Churches, especially those of an evangelical persuasion, receive spiritual nourishment is through hearing, and obeying, God's word in the

> *There is no place for a priestly hierarchy in the Church.*
>
> HARVEY COX,
> NORTH AMERICAN THEOLOGIAN

Bible. In the main services the preaching of the Bible is of prime importance. Prayers are

A choir in a Pentecostal Church in South Africa displaying the lively and enthusiastic worship characteristic of the denomination.

Quaker meetings are quiet and meditative. Anyone who senses that God is prompting them will speak to the group.

The sharing of personal testimonies or experiences of God may feature in some meetings.

said, usually spontaneous ones, passages are read from the Bible, hymns are sung and a sermon is preached.

In charismatic Evangelical Churches the leadership may encourage freedom and spontaneity in worship. This can take the form of praying or singing 'in tongues', prophecies, spontaneous singing, personal testimony or prayers for members of the fellowship. The emphasis of such worship is on openness to the prompting of

LEADERSHIP

The leadership of a worship service depends on the denomination. Some Churches have an appointed minister but in others the leadership is non-ordained, or 'lay'. Lay leadership is particularly common in house churches, which try to avoid any suggestion of a church hierarchy. In Catholic, Orthodox and Anglican Churches, only a priest can perform certain ceremonies, such as the consecration of the bread and wine at the Eucharist.

the Holy Spirit rather than following a prescribed pattern of worship or liturgy. While many Roman Catholics are part of the charismatic renewal movement, such freedom of expression is unlikely in the Sunday Mass. Catholic charismatics normally meet informally in weekly prayer and worship groups.

Baptism and Confirmation

Baptism is usually performed on infants, although some Churches baptize adults. Confirmation tends to take place in early adolescence.

For Christians, immersion in the waters of baptism symbolizes their participation in Jesus' death. Their sins are buried, and they are raised out of the water to new life through the power of Christ's resurrection. Baptism involves either full immersion in water or pouring sanctified water (which represents purification) on the candidate's head while invoking the three persons of the Holy Trinity, Father, Son and Holy Spirit.

Infant baptism

Many Christians are baptized as infants, with parents and godparents taking vows on their behalf. Godparents are chosen by the parents and entrusted with the responsibility of ensuring that the child is brought up in the Christian faith. Parents and godparents gather around the font as the priest challenges them about the strength of their own Christian faith by asking them several prescribed questions. The priest uses water from the font to make the 'sign of the cross',

a symbol of the death of Christ, on the baby's forehead before naming it and baptizing it 'in the name of the Father and of the Son and of the Holy Spirit'.

Roman Catholics and some

The service of infant baptism welcomes the child into the Church family. A State Church christening in Germany.

Anglicans rub blessed oil (chrism) on the baby's forehead to show that the Holy Spirit has come to the child through baptism. The priest may also take a candle lit from a large paschal candle and hand it to the parents with the words, 'Receive this light. This is to show that you have passed from darkness to light.' The baby is then welcomed into the fellowship of the Church. When the child is much older, he or she can return for confirmation, a conscious and personal commitment to the Christian faith.

In the Orthodox Church, after blessing the water in the font with a prayer and breathing on it, the priest anoints the baby with the 'oil of gladness'. The baby is undressed, placed in the font facing eastwards and immersed in the water three times. The ceremony of chrismation, the Orthodox equivalent of confirmation, occurs almost immediately afterwards with the baby being anointed on the forehead, eyes, nose, ears and mouth with consecrated chrism.

Since the time of the early Church the laying on of hands has been linked with confirmation and praying for the sick.

Believer's baptism

Some Protestant denominations,

> *Baptismal grace, the presence of the Holy Spirit — inalienable and personal to each one of us — is the foundation of all Christian life.*
>
> VLADIMIR LOSSKY,
> RUSSIAN-BORN THEOLOGIAN

especially Baptists, believe that infant baptism has little basis in the Bible and that a baby cannot make a conscious decision to repent and be converted as suggested in the ceremony. Baptists and other groups, therefore, reserve baptism for adults and this takes the form of a public confession of faith and full immersion in water.

For the first two centuries of the Church's existence baptism was universally for adult believers only. Between the third and the seventh centuries infant baptism became the norm but believer's baptism reappeared with the birth of the Baptist Church at the beginning of the 17th century.

Believer's baptism is a means of publicly confessing faith in Christ. The believer is fully immersed in water as a graphic reminder of his identification with the death, burial and resurrection of Jesus.

Weddings and Funerals

All Christians see marriage as a serious commitment, and wedding vows are made before God. Christians believe strongly that death is not the end and this is reflected in their funeral services.

Marriage and family life are highly valued within Christianity, although many traditions respect those who remain single, whether laypeople, members of a religious community or priests. Some traditions, such as the Roman Catholic Church, do not recognize divorce.

Wedding services

In the Orthodox and Catholic Churches marriage is a sacrament. The Orthodox marriage service is full of symbolism to show that it is Christ who unites and blesses the couple, since it is in his presence that the promises are made and the rings exchanged. Uniquely in the Orthodox service, the priest crowns the bride and groom with wreaths to show that they have become king and queen over their own kingdom of the family, which mirrors the kingdom of God. They are also remembering those martyrs who have borne the same witness to the Christian faith as they will bear in their married life. To symbolize their unity they share a glass of wine and join hands as they walk three times around the central table.

In the Catholic Church, the marriage service takes place within the context of a nuptial Mass. It is the couple, not the

The teaching of Jesus on the indissolubility of marriage is not absolutely clear and the attitude of the different Churches towards divorce is also mixed.

priest, who give the bread and wine to each other and this makes the Catholic service unique.

In most Protestant Churches, the service is led by an ordained minister and the couple exchange vows. Communion is not usually part of the service, the emphasis being more on readings from the Bible and on the sermon preached by the minister.

Christians believe that Christ has defeated death. As a result, the soul lives on beyond the grave in an unbreakable union with God. Funeral at Hammaus Kraal, South Africa.

Between the fourth and eighth centuries the Church's attitude towards funerals changed. In the fourth century funerals were occasions for joy and everyone wore white. By the eighth century the prayers were for a speedy release from hell (purgatory) and everyone wore black.

Funerals

There are references in the New Testament to anointing the sick with oil. Called unction, this is continued today in some traditions, notably the Roman Catholic Church in which extreme unction is offered to the dying, while praying for forgiveness of sins.

Christians believe that the soul lives for ever after death, and that at the end of time the body will be resurrected to share in Christ's own victory over death. These two beliefs are central to the funeral services of all Christian denominations.

In the Protestant Churches, the funeral service includes hymns, prayers, Bible readings and a short eulogy. This is followed by the committal, a second service which is held at the graveside, in which the person's body is committed to the earth and God's safe keeping. The committal may also take place at a crematorium.

In the Catholic Church the coffin is often taken to the church on the night before the funeral so that prayers can be said for the soul of the dead person. A Catholic funeral service is called a Requiem Mass.

In the Orthodox tradition an open coffin is positioned at the front of the church. The coffin remains open during the service to remind everyone that death is not an unnecessary tragedy; it is God's punishment for sin. The hope of the resurrection is symbolized by the candles that burn throughout the service and the incense that is sprinkled over the coffin. The body of the deceased is anointed and blessed with holy oil and the service ends with those present taking their farewell with a kiss.

Christmas

The Christian year begins with the first Sunday in Advent, the last Sunday in November. There are four Sundays in Advent leading up to Christmas Day. Some Churches also celebrate Epiphany on 6th January.

No one knows for sure when Jesus was born. It was not until the fourth century, during the time of Emperor Constantine, that the event was celebrated on 25 December. This was the time when the Roman festival celebrating the birth of Mithras (the Unconquerable Sun) on this date was Christianized.

Advent is a time of preparation for the season of Christmas. The early Christians did not celebrate Advent, or the birth of Jesus at Christmas, and it was not until the sixth century that Christians began to set aside a time to remember the coming of the Messiah into the stable at Bethlehem.

> *The ox and the ass understood more of the first Christmas than the High Priests in Jerusalem. And it is the same today.*
>
> THOMAS MERTON (1915–68), NORTH AMERICAN CISTERCIAN MONK AND WRITER

Three comings

During Advent Christians recall three comings:

◆ the coming of John the Baptist, who is presented in the Gospels as God's messenger, the one sent ahead to prepare the people for the coming of Jesus.
◆ the coming of the Messiah. This coming was foretold throughout the Old Testament by many of the prophets but the one who saw events most clearly was Isaiah. Readings from the book of Isaiah figure prominently during Advent.
◆ the Second Coming of Jesus, the Son of God, to be the Judge at the end of the age.

Christmas time

During the season of Christmas itself carols are sung and in some countries churches stage pageants re-enacting the story of Jesus' birth. It is traditional to put an evergreen tree up inside the home, decorated with lights and ornaments. Some Christians gather on Christmas Eve for a

Many Churches make rich use of symbolism in their worship during the season of Advent.

The festival of Epiphany celebrates the visit of the Magi to the infant Jesus, and also looks forward to the Second Coming of Jesus. An Epiphany procession of the Ethiopian Orthodox Church in Addis Ababa.

In the West Advent lasts for four Sundays but in the Orthodox Churches it is a longer festival beginning in the middle of November. In the East Advent is still kept as a fast, although less strictly than Lent.

candlelit service, and on Christmas Day, Protestant and Catholic children are often encouraged to believe that presents are magically brought

THE CHRISTIAN CALENDAR

The system of numbering years most common in the Western world is based on the year when it was thought that Jesus was born. AD stands for *Anno Domini*, the 'year of our Lord', and BC stands for 'before Christ'. However, recent research reveals that Jesus was probably born in 4 BCE, not 1 CE. The 'Christian' dating system only became widespread after the eighth century. Up till then the Church had numbered its years from the date of the foundation of Rome – 753 BCE.

by St Nicholas, also known as Santa Claus or Father Christmas, a fourth-century bishop known for his generosity. Many families share a celebratory meal on either Christmas Eve or Christmas Day.

Epiphany

The Christmas season ends with the feast of Epiphany or Candlemas. Epiphany means 'manifestation' or 'showing forth' and commemorates the three manifestations of Jesus – to the wise men who travelled from the East, to the people at his baptism and to his disciples at his transfiguration.

Easter

The liturgical cycle of Easter celebrates the events that led up to Christ's crucifixion. It begins with the 40-day period of Lent on Ash Wednesday and ends with the holiest Christian festival of all on Easter Day.

Liturgically, Easter is preceded by Lent, a 40-day period of repentance and fasting. In the Orthodox tradition Lent is preceded by four extra weeks called the Great Fast, during which many worshippers follow ancient rules, abstaining from eating any meat and animal products, and only eating fish on certain days. The biblical precedent for Lent comes from the time Jesus spent in the wilderness being tempted by Satan. Matthew tells us that Jesus was actually led into the wilderness, directly after his baptism, by the Spirit of God, to be tempted for 40 days.

In the West, Lent begins with Ash Wednesday, the day after Shrove Tuesday, when many Christians have ash smudged on their foreheads by a priest who says, 'Dust thou art and unto dust thou shalt return.'

Holy Week

On the Sunday before Easter (Palm Sunday) Jesus'

The word 'Maundy' comes from the first word of the traditional Latin anthem for Maundy Thursday, *Mandatum novum do vobis*, which means, 'A new commandment I give you.' The new commandment that Jesus gave to his disciples at the Last Supper was, 'Love one another as I have loved you.'

Since 1955 Good Friday and Holy Saturday have been the only days in the Christian year on which the Mass is not celebrated in Roman Catholic Churches.

Re-enactment of biblical events is a feature of Christianity in some countries. Preparing for a Palm Sunday procession in Mompós, Colombia.

THE GREAT VIGIL

In Russia, the Great Vigil to welcome Easter morning lasts from midnight until dawn and the people stand for the whole service.

Here is a description of such a service from a church in Kiev, where 2,000 people were packed into the church and the same number stood outside:

The dean went out the royal doors into the congregation and sang out, 'Christos voskresye! (Christ is risen!)' Everyone responded in one voice, 'Veyeastino voskresye! (Truly he is risen!)' It is impossible to put on paper how this sounds in the dead of night in a church overheated by crowds of people and hundreds of candles. It is like a shudder in the earth, the cracking open of the tomb. Then there was an explosion of ringing bells.

JIM FOREST, *PILGRIM TO THE RUSSIAN CHURCH*

The pageantry and ritual of the Russian Orthodox Church is illustrated by this Easter procession around the monastery at Tobolsk in Siberia.

The Saxons called March *lencten monath* because in this month the days lengthen noticeably. As the main part of the 40-day fast occurs in March it was given the name *Lencten faesten*, or Lent.

triumphant entry into Jerusalem is commemorated by the waving of palm branches in churches and the shouting of 'Hosanna!' On Maundy Thursday Christians remember the Last Supper when Jesus instituted the Communion, or Eucharist, by breaking bread and drinking wine. On Good Friday Jesus' death is mourned and most churches hold special services of remembrance. The pain of Good Friday gives way to the joy of Easter Sunday when Jesus' resurrection is celebrated.

Some churches hold a vigil service on Easter Saturday evening to anticipate Christ's emergence from the tomb.

Pentecost

The festival of Easter brings to a close the two main cycles in the Christian year, but there remains the festival of Pentecost when Christians remember the giving of the Holy Spirit to the disciples.

Ascension Day comes 40 days after Easter Day and marks the occasion when Jesus left the disciples for the last time and returned to his Father in heaven. Ascension Day is a holy day in the Catholic Church and is always celebrated by a Mass. It is a time for encouraging Christians to look forward a further 10 days to the celebration of Pentecost.

A Jewish festival

Pentecost is a Jewish festival held on the 50th day after Passover. Also called Shavuot, Pentecost commemorates the giving of the Ten Commandments to Moses on Mount Sinai. The Holy Spirit was poured out on the apostles during Pentecost, so Christians

> We must each of us be humbled by this fresh wind of the Spirit that has come to lift us up from the nadir our civilization has reached.
>
> GEORGE MACLEOD,
> SCOTTISH PRESBYTERIAN
> MINISTER AND FOUNDER OF
> THE IONA COMMUNITY

THE TRANSFIGURATION AND THE ASSUMPTION

Some Christian Churches celebrate two further feast days. On 6 August Christians remember the transfiguration of Jesus on the mountain top when he revealed his supernatural radiance. On 15 August, the Catholic and Orthodox Churches celebrate the assumption of Mary, known as the 'Falling Asleep of the Mother of God'. Both these feasts feature strongly in the Eastern Orthodox Church, which tends to put greater emphasis on the ability of humanity to break out of its worldly chains and rise into the light than on the darkness of sin.

It was a custom in the early 20th century for walks to be held over the Pentecost weekend, during which Christians sought to share their faith with others.

celebrate the Day of Pentecost in remembrance of this pivotal event in the Church.

In the Orthodox Church a memorial service is held on the Day of Pentecost to remember dead believers. Worshippers bring food to the service, which

> *The Holy Spirit is the source of community and the Spirit's work is more related to the building of community than to the edification of the isolated individual.*
>
> JIM WALLIS, NORTH AMERICAN CHRISTIAN ACTIVIST, WRITER AND FOUNDER OF THE SOJOURNERS COMMUNITY

has a strong affinity to the Catholic service of All Souls.

In the Western Church, Pentecost is often called Whitsun, literally 'white Sunday', recalling the time in the early Church when people wore white garments for the baptismal ceremonies that were performed at this time of year and for some time afterwards.

Pentecost is also taken as the birthday of the Church, the time when the disciples were empowered to go out from Jerusalem and spread the gospel of Jesus Christ.

Pentecost by Barnaba da Modena (active 1361–83).

In the 20th century, Christianity declined in some parts of the world but gained members and vitality in others. This trend continues in the 21st century.

In Protestantism, traditional denominations in the USA and Europe are losing members not so much because of their teachings but because they seem uninspiring and irrelevant to the majority of people. George Carey, the archbishop of Canterbury, feels that Christian teaching is less and less likely to be taken into account when people are making moral choices and he fears that in England God is 'being banished to the realm of the private hobby'.

Roman Catholicism is becoming increasingly divided between conservatives and liberals. After the greater openness engendered by the Second Vatican Council (1962–65), Pope John Paul II has refocused attention on the more traditional and conservative teachings of the Church. He has travelled extensively, urging a return to traditional family values. The Catholic Church is struggling in many

In recent years church growth in South Korea has been phenomenal. Young Nak Presbyterian Church, Seoul.

parts of the world to attract men to the priesthood, and in some Western countries there is growing pressure for the acceptance of women priests. Among other challenges facing the Church are birth control, abortion, surrogate motherhood, genetic engineering, divorce and homosexuality.

Other less traditional groups and movements are thriving, however. These include evangelical, pentecostal and charismatic movements, the ministry of healing, radical social justice groups and non-Western Churches.

> *Nothing is more needed by humanity today, and by the Church in particular, than the recovery of a sense of 'beyondness' in the whole of life to revive the springs of wonder and adoration.*
>
> JOHN V. TAYLOR,
> ENGLISH ANGLICAN BISHOP

CONTEMPORARY CHRISTIANITY

Contents

Evangelicals

The 20th century saw a rapid growth in the number of evangelical Christians. To evangelize is to preach the good news of Jesus and encourage people to become Christians in the light of this. Evangelical Christians emphasize the importance of the Bible, the saving grace of God through Jesus Christ and the missionary imperative of the gospel.

The current evangelical movement can be traced back to the fundamentalist—modernist controversy of the early 20th century. The fundamentalists opposed the liberal or modern stream in Christianity that tried to bring science and religion together and to understand the Bible through historical and archaeological research. They called for a return to the 'fundamentals', which they identified as:

◆ the inspiration and authority of scripture.
◆ the virgin birth of Christ and his miracles.
◆ the divinity of Christ and the literal truth of the resurrection.
◆ Christ's death which atoned for the sins of all.
◆ belief in the literal and imminent Second Coming of Christ.

During the 20th century this fundamentalist movement

Throughout the world, evangelists have conveyed the message of the good news of Jesus.

Billy Graham has been speaking to huge audiences for over 50 years, challenging them to respond to the message of the love of Jesus. He has been heard speaking in person by more people than any other individual in history.

BILLY GRAHAM

The American Billy Graham is the most successful Christian evangelist in history and his converts number millions.

Graham uses modern mass communication and organization to convey a simple gospel message. He stresses individual decisions for Christ and careful follow-up to integrate new believers into churches. In recent years evangelists have increasingly used all forms of modern media, such as television and the internet, to spread the gospel.

blossomed into what is now known as the evangelical movement. Evangelicals are prominent in many Protestant denominations, and are particularly known for their stress on Bible study, their teaching that people are 'born again' when they become Christians, their development of strong personal relationships with Christ, sharing their faith with others and their focus on the Church as the vibrant people of God. There are differences, however, between evangelicals: some, for example, are more conservative on theological and ethical issues than others.

Evangelicalism is having an increasing impact in South America, a continent that is largely Roman Catholic as a result of Spanish and Portuguese colonization in the 15th and 16th centuries. In the early 1990s an average of five Evangelical Churches were being set up each week in Rio de Janeiro, many in the slum areas.

Pentecostals and Charismatics

The 20th century saw the rise of the Pentecostal denominations, and charismatic renewal has been a more recent movement. Both groups have grown rapidly and up to one quarter of all Christians can now be considered members of the Pentecostal-charismatic movement.

Pentecostalism is characterized by its emphasis on 'baptism in the Holy Spirit'. The outward sign of this is a manifestation of the spiritual gifts that Paul lists in 1 Corinthians 12. These gifts include prophecy, healing and speaking in tongues and have their antecedent in the events of the Day of Pentecost, when the Holy Spirit descended on the disciples, empowering them and enabling them to speak in foreign languages. Pentecostals derive their name from this day.

The Azusa Street revival

The crucial event in the development of Pentecostalism occurred in the USA in a storefront church on Azusa Street, Los Angeles, in 1906. Here William Seymour (1870–1922), a black preacher, taught his mixed congregation about baptism in the Holy Spirit and speaking in tongues. From there, the new movement spread rapidly through North and South America and Europe,

and had an effect on newly emerging churches in Africa. Pentecostal Churches became known for their freedom of

The storefront church in Azusa Street, Los Angeles, in 1906, where the modern Pentecostal movement had its beginnings.

Pentecostals and charismatics are now the fastest-growing groups in the Church worldwide.

This moment when you really feel God's power in yourself brings so much peace and joy within you. It transforms you and society. There comes a sense of total forgiveness for your sins, and the ability in you to forgive others. At that moment, you start to speak in different languages, maybe such that no one can understand... The main thing is that the person should be filled with God's Power. A nice-looking car will not move unless it is fuelled. God's Power will only fill those who are pure. That is why in the early Church people went into the wilderness to fast and repent. Then God could fill them with his Power. Each sermon should have this Power of God; then the people will really listen and repent of their sins.

ROMAN BILAS, HEAD OF THE UNION OF PENTECOSTAL
CHRISTIANS OF EVANGELICAL FAITH, MOSCOW

expression in worship and an openness to contributions from all worshippers. The sometimes extreme emotionalism associated with the movement led to the nickname, 'Holy Rollers'.

Charismatic renewal

Although Pentecostalism started off as multiracial, it quickly separated into largely black or white churches. Pentecostal congregations were often despised by the traditional Churches because their membership tended to be poor and badly educated. Eventually, though, the movement became accepted by mainstream denominations, giving birth to what is known as charismatic renewal. The word 'charismatic' comes from 'charismata' referring to the gifts of the Spirit. Charismatic renewal has affected all the traditional denominations and has probably had its greatest impact among Roman Catholics. Pentecostals and charismatics are now the fastest-growing groups in Christianity worldwide.

Healing

Pentecostalism and charismatic renewal have been largely responsible for the development of healing ministries in recent times. Previously it had not been common to pray for healing, and miraculous cures tended to be associated only with saints.

Nowadays many Christians will pray for healing at some stage in their lives – whether for themselves or for someone else. The popularity of charismatic renewal has led to a recovery of the gift of healing, and many Churches, especially those within evangelical and charismatic traditions, hold special healing services or encourage members of the congregation to pray for healing. This often involves the 'laying

Many churches regard healing as evidence of God's activity as well as his compassion.

The Virgin Mary appeared to Bernadette Soubiroux at Lourdes in 1858. Many now come here seeking healing.

PSYCHOLOGY AND HEALING

As psychology developed in the early part of the 20th century, Christians were generally mistrustful of the new science. For their part, psychologists and psychoanalysts often portrayed religion as unscientific and harmful to human well-being. Today things are much improved and the two disciplines are more sympathetic towards each other. Christians are increasingly aware of the value of psychological concepts and therapies in helping them understand the complexity of the human person created by God. One of the most influential psychologists has been Carl G. Jung (1875–1961). The son of a minister, Jung was born and spent much of his life in Switzerland. Among his most significant insights are those of the unconscious and the collective unconscious with its archetypes, the stages of life, the masculine and feminine sides of personality and the 'shadow' or dark side of human beings.

on of hands' so that the person praying actually touches the person they are praying for.

Healing mind, body and soul

In the USA, the most influential person in the healing movement was Agnes Sanford (1897–1976). She emphasized the importance of emotional as well as physical healing and wrote a number of books on the subject. She coined the term 'healing of the memories' for an emotional release from past wounds through the reimaging of the event in the presence of Jesus. Another American, Francis MacNutt (1925–), wrote a best-selling book in 1974 simply called *Healing*. He distinguished four types of healing: spiritual, physical, emotional and deliverance from evil spirits.

Healing at pilgrimage sites

Within the Roman Catholic and Orthodox Churches healings are usually associated with particular places of pilgrimage. The most popular are sites of apparitions of the Virgin Mary. Mary appeared to Juan Diego in Guadeloupe, Mexico, in 1531 and to Bernadette Soubiroux at Lourdes, France, in 1858. Both sites are now extremely popular with pilgrims seeking spiritual help and healing.

> *Good theology makes good psychology.*
>
> M. SCOTT PECK, AMERICAN PSYCHIATRIST AND AUTHOR

The Ecumenical Movement

In the 20th century concerted efforts were made to heal the rifts between the various Christian denominations. Christians are now seeking to unite around areas of agreement or at least to enjoy fellowship with each other. And in the process many people are discovering riches in traditions they previously ignored.

The Second Vatican Council (1962–65) asserted that the Roman Catholic Church is the one Church of Christ, but it also opened the way for dialogue with other strands of Christianity by affirming that the Holy Spirit was working in them as well. The Orthodox Church similarly believes that it

One outcome of the Second Vatican Council was the greater freedom given to Roman Catholics to recognize and engage in fellowship with Christians from other traditions.

Pope John Paul II encouraged forgiveness and unity between denominations.

Meeting of the World Council of Churches at Cathédrale St Pierre, Geneva.

alone is the 'one, holy, catholic and apostolic Church'. While it seeks the union of all Christians, it stresses the importance of uniformity in questions of faith. Roman Catholic and Orthodox Churches do not, therefore, share Communion with those beyond their respective denominations. Some Protestant denominations also refuse to recognize each other's validity.

New hope?

However, in 1995 Pope John Paul II issued an encyclical called, 'That They May All Be One', in which he encouraged Roman Catholics, Protestants, Anglicans and Orthodox Christians to forgive each other for past hurts and mistakes so that the followers of Christ could be reunited. More recent pronouncements by the Pope have, however, been seen by Protestants as less encouraging, and in reality much of the effective ecumenism has occurred at a local, grass-roots level rather than at the top.

The World Council of Churches was formed in 1948 with the aim of helping Christians to collaborate on service projects despite their theological differences. It is the main ecumenical body for Protestant, Orthodox, Lutheran and Anglican traditions and its Faith and Order Commission brings together 300 very different Christian Churches worldwide to wrestle with the challenges of Christian unity.

> *There are three gestures, in particular, which are capable of being signs of God at work, paths of communion and ways of discovering new dimensions of ecumenism: avoid separating the generations; go to meet those who cannot believe; stand alongside the exploited.*
>
> ROGER OF TAIZÉ,
> CO-FOUNDER AND PRIOR OF THE
> TAIZÉ COMMUNITY IN FRANCE

Culture

Up until the 20th century the dominant Christian culture was a European and an American one. With the spread of the gospel to all corners of the planet, however, this Western Christian culture has been questioned and in many countries discarded altogether.

As the 21st century progresses Christianity will no longer be a religion of the West. The centre of gravity is moving to Africa, Latin America and parts of Asia.

Cultural heritage

When evangelizing the world many Western Christians believed that their particular brand of Christianity was the right one and they often expected the people they helped convert to become replicas of themselves. However, newly created Christian communities have often reacted against such cultural imperialism and tried to detach themselves from the cultural baggage the Westerners brought with them. They have wanted to restore the validity of their own cultural heritage, and indeed the insights of many non-Western Christians have enriched the Church worldwide.

In Asia, Christians, who are usually in the minority, stress a Christ who is present in the

The old-style missionaries usually brought good healthcare and education with them, as well as the gospel, but they were too closely associated with colonialism. However, since many countries have gained political independence, local Christians are re-evaluating the gospel so that it is more in tune with local culture.
An English missionary in Malaya around 1910.

The European-style architecture of Lusaka Cathedral, Zambia. The remnants of colonialism seem increasingly inappropriate to many indigenous people.

The new-style missionary treats local people as equals. An Irish missionary talks with a Masai man in Kenya.

whole of the universe and who invites all people to share in his love at a common table. In Africa, the independent Churches have frequently brought their traditional ways of celebrating — drumming, dancing and singing — into community worship. They find it helpful to see Jesus as the greatest of ancestors, a mediator between human beings and the divine. In Latin America, Christian communities like to call Jesus the liberator from oppression as well as the more traditional Saviour.

Here is an extract from *The Poisonwood Bible* which tells the story of a fierce American Baptist minister and his family arriving in Africa as missionaries. This passage is narrated by Rachel, one of the daughters:

And the beat of my heart was not my heart, I finally figured out, but the drums. The men were pounding on big loggedy-looking drums, and women were singing high, quavery tunes like birds gone crazy in the full moon. They called the songs back and forth in their own language between a leader and the rest of the group. They were such weird songs it took me a while to realize they followed the tunes of Christian hymns, 'Onward Christian Soldiers' and 'What a

Friend I Have in Jesus', which made my skin crawl. I guess they have a right to sing them, but here's the thing: right in front of our very eyes, some of the women stood up there in the firelight with their bosoms naked as a jaybird's egg... I kept glancing over at Father, wondering, Am I the only one getting shocked to smithereens here? He had that narrow-eyed, lockjawed look like he was starting to get steamed up, but you never know exactly where that's going to lead. Mostly someplace where you wish you were anyplace but.

BARBARA KINGSOLVER, *THE POISONWOOD BIBLE*

Social Transformation

While for some Christians the practice of their faith is largely a private matter, for others commitment to the gospel demands an involvement in politics and social issues. For these Christians, the incarnation of God in the person of Jesus shows the depth of God's participation in the affairs of the world. They believe that they, too, must be politically and socially engaged.

Social justice is a strong theme in the Bible, in both the Old and New Testaments. Many of the Old Testament prophets, for example, speak of God's justice and of his concern for the poor and the disadvantaged. In the New Testament, Jesus' teaching and lifestyle were radical and fully engaged with society; in contrast, for example, with the existing patriarchal society around him with its proscriptions of impurity, Jesus healed lepers and a bleeding woman by touching them. He willingly ate with people of all social classes and seemed especially to seek out the 'sinners and tax collectors'. In a culture that severely restricted the role of women, Jesus welcomed women as disciples. He was egalitarian and inclusive in his approach and he spelled this out in his teaching in the Sermon on the Mount.

The ministry of Jesus demonstrated God's compassion for the poor, the sick and the oppressed. The church has often been in the forefront of providing care for those in need. Patients await treatment at an eye hospital in India

I have a dream that my four little children will one day live in a nation where they will not be judged by the colour of their skin but by the content of their character.

MARTIN LUTHER KING
(1929–68), AFRICAN-
AMERICAN CIVIL
RIGHTS LEADER

Martin Luther King was prominent in campaigning for the civil rights of black Americans during the 1960s. His beliefs arose from his conviction that all people were equal in the sight of God.

Martin Luther King

Throughout history, Christians have sought to live out the implications of Jesus' teaching. In the contemporary world, the search for social justice takes many forms. The USA, for example, saw the fight against racial injustice led by Martin Luther King, a Baptist preacher, until his assassination in 1968. The African-American community that King represented so effectively is predominantly Christian and has been nourished down the ages by a spirituality of endurance, liberation and celebration. The sufferings of African-Americans from slavery and discrimination have created a community that is bonded together through heartfelt worship in which music and preaching are central.

Liberation theology

In Latin America, liberation theology developed from the 1960s onwards and has influenced Christians across the world. Liberation theology stresses the need for political action and involvement to help the poor.

Desmond Tutu

In South Africa, Christians were in the forefront of the fight to end the oppressive regime of apartheid. They were led by the Anglican Archbishop of Cape Town, Desmond Tutu, whose fearless stand for truth and justice won him the Nobel Peace Prize in 1984.

141

Persecution

In many countries today, Christians are experiencing persecution, and in some cases death, for their faith.

No reliable figures exist for the number of Christians who have been persecuted or have lost their lives in the modern era but it is considerable. Among the places where Christians have suffered noticeably are China, Pakistan and Sudan.

China

After the victory of the Communists in the 1940s the Three-Self Patriotic Movement was founded to make the Church in China truly national. Other Churches with foreign links were banned. The Cultural Revolution in 1966 led to churches being destroyed and desecrated, with priests, pastors and laypeople imprisoned and tortured. Isolated and brutally persecuted, the Christian Church seemed to be on the verge of extinction, but, despite a systematic policy of ruthless extermination, Christian groups continued to function underground.

The end of the Cultural Revolution in 1969 and the death of Mao Tse-Tung in 1976 led to the reopening of some churches, but persecution continues nonetheless. Hundreds of Chinese Christians, ranging from evangelical house-church members and teachers to Roman Catholic priests and bishops have found themselves in 're-education-through-labour' camps. In the late 1990s Amnesty International reported cases from China of Christian women being hung by their thumbs from wires, beaten with heavy rods, denied food and water and shocked with electric probes.

Pakistan

In Pakistan in recent years, many Christians have been imprisoned and tortured for preaching their faith. In this society, respect for civil and political rights deteriorated significantly after the bloodless military coup on 12 October 1999, and religious minorities have suffered abuses. The country's blasphemy law means that anything that can be construed as speech directed against the Prophet Muhammed is punishable with stringent penalties, and in May 2000 a lower court in Sialkot district, Punjab, sentenced two Christian

The case of the Christian brother arrested for blasphemy against Muhammed was reportedly registered by an ice-cream vendor who had fought with the brothers after insisting that his dishes were reserved for Muslim customer only.

Authorities in China have banned meetings of unregistered churches. Those who would not comply have been the victims of brutal and persistent persecution. But official efforts at control have led to the creation of a massive underground Church, which appears to be growing at a phenomenal speed.

brothers to 35 years' imprisonment and a fine of 1,500 US dollars. They were convicted of desecrating the Qur'an and blaspheming against the Prophet Muhammed.

Sudan

In many ways the situation in the Muslim country of Sudan is worse than anywhere else. The Sudanese government has undertaken a programme of forced conversion to the faith of Islam. Many of the black Sudanese in the south of the country (the north is largely

> *They found out that I was a Christian... They wanted me to 'confess' at a public meeting. I refused. So they smashed everything in the house, burnt my Bible, my hymnbook — and then made me eat the ashes. They cut my hair, slung placards over my front and back and made me collect the night-soil.*
>
> CHINESE LAYPERSON DURING THE CULTURAL REVOLUTION

Arab) have resisted such conversion, often because of their commitment to Christianity — a criminal act under Sudanese law. To punish them the government has denied food to people living in areas of famine and has sold many Christian children, some as young as six, into slavery.

Ecology

In the 20th and 21st centuries humanity has become increasingly concerned about the natural world and its role in enhancing or destroying it. Some blame Christianity for the erosion of the environment, pointing to the text in the book of Genesis that exhorts humankind to have dominion over the natural world. Others blame industrial progress and commercial competition. An increasing number of Christians now believe it is their responsibility to take an active interest in protecting the natural world.

While Western countries have often exploited natural resources for profit, many of the indigenous cultures of the world view nature differently. They believe that the divine spirit lives everywhere, that everything is sacred and that human beings are only part of the great circle of life.

Many Christians are learning from such ancient beliefs and advocating a greater respect towards the natural world. There is also increasing recognition of the miracle of creation and this in turn is helping to unite science and religion. Key figures in this process include Pierre Teilhard de Chardin (1881–1955), Albert Schweitzer (1875–1965) and Pope John Paul II. The latter called Francis of Assisi, the 14th-century Italian saint

known, among other things, for his love of animals, the patron saint of ecology.

Francis of Assisi has been called the patron saint of ecology. *Saint Francis Preaching to the Birds* by Giotto di Bondone (c. 1266–1337)

PIERRE TEILHARD DE CHARDIN

Pierre Teilhard de Chardin (1881–1955), a Jesuit priest, did more than any other 20th-century spiritual writer to direct people's minds to creation and thereby to the relationship between science and religion. De Chardin was one of the first 'creation-centred' Christians and he saw the mind of God in the perfect, intricate balances of chemistry, biology and physics that allow life to exist. De Chardin's books, however, were censored by the Catholic Church and for most of his life he was forbidden to publish. It was only after his death that his work became widespread and influential.

> *I bless you matter, and you I acclaim: not as the pontiffs of science or the moralizing preachers depict you, debased, disfigured — as mass of brute forces and base appetites — but as you reveal yourself to me today, in your totality and your true nature.*
>
> PIERRE TEILHARD DE CHARDIN (1881–1955), 'HYMN TO MATTER'

The greed and materialism of the developed nations brought about a massive destruction of natural resources during the 20th century. God's mandate to human beings to manage his world has been selfishly disregarded for apparently short-term gain.

Matthew Fox

Another person whose theology has aroused interest as well as suspicion is Matthew Fox (1940–), who was expelled from the Dominican Order and the Catholic priesthood in 1993 and became an Episcopal priest in San Francisco in 1994. Fox is associated with creation-centred spirituality, which includes appreciation of the feminine aspect of God and celebration of the human body as blessed. Fox speaks of 'original blessing' rather than 'original sin'.

Feminism

Increasing numbers of women across the world are reacting against what they perceive as a male-dominated Church. Women of colour have sometimes distanced themselves from the word 'feminist', preferring 'womanist' or *muhajarista* theologies to express the distinctive characteristics of their struggle.

While the Church has historically been patriarchal, there is good evidence that Jesus had female disciples and that there were women leaders in the early churches. Feminist theology has, therefore, tried to reconstruct the history of women in the early days of Christianity, and to examine the effects of male domination. There are three main areas of feminist theology:

Does the New Testament fail to portray Mary as a person in her own right? *Madonna Litta* by Leonardo da Vinci (1452–1519).

◆ examination of the New Testament, especially the writings of the apostle Paul. Some of the statements in Paul's letters to the first Christian communities seem oppressive to women; others seem egalitarian. For example, he argues that men should pray or prophesy with their heads uncovered but that women should cover their heads so as not to reveal their hair.

◆ examination of the role models for women given in the Bible. Mary, Mother of Jesus, is the principal female in the New Testament and for many her portrayal in scripture is a stumbling block, not just because she seems to represent the ideals of purity and submissiveness, but also paradoxically because she seems primarily defined by

THE ORDINATION OF WOMEN

In many Reformed Churches, women are able to become ministers and to lead congregations. However, in the Roman Catholic and Eastern Orthodox Churches, ordination is only open to men. Increasing

numbers of women, especially in the Roman Catholic Church, are voicing their opposition to this restriction. In the Anglican Church, the decision to admit women to the priesthood in November 1992 was hailed as a major breakthrough by women's groups, but greeted with dismay by traditionalists who believe the Bible and Church tradition forbid women to act as priests at the Eucharist and thereby represent the male Christ. Some conservative evangelicals also have difficulty with the notion of women in leadership positions, arguing that the Bible places men at the head.

A woman priest administering communion in Biskopshaven Church, Norway.

her maternalism rather than as a person in her own right, the Virgin Mary being a name often used to describe her.

◆ the idea of God. The Christian Church refers to God as 'he' or 'Father', but scholarship shows that this patriarchal usage is not absolute: there were also other images of God as mother, divine wisdom, justice, friend and lover.

Sexuality

One of the most difficult issues facing the contemporary Church is that of human sexuality. In recent years the growing tolerance, especially in the West, towards homosexuality has led to greater pressure for a more open attitude to homosexuals within the Churches. The issue has become divisive for many Churches and the debate shows no sign of resolution.

Since the early days of the Church, Christians have been ambivalent about the human body: on the one hand it has often been seen as a burden to be suffered; on the other hand it is the crucial material out of which devotional practice and spiritual progress are forged. Thus the body has traditionally been honoured and cared for as well as endured and disciplined.

Celebration of the body

With the rise in recent years of creation-centred spirituality and the growth of the Christian ecology movement, the body has been viewed in a more positive light. Much spiritual writing in the latter part of the 20th century onwards has promoted the recovery of sensual embodiment in the world and encouraged Christians to reflect on the full meaning of Christ's physical incarnation. Such teaching has been particularly prominent in the gay and lesbian movement which has developed in the last 50 years or so, and from this movement emerges one of the thorniest issues currently facing Christian denominations.

Homosexuality

Traditional Christian teaching is that heterosexual relationships are the norm and that sexual expression of love between a man and a woman should be within marriage. While homosexual orientation is not condemned, sexual acts between those of the same sex are outlawed, and verses from the Bible

The Old Testament hero David is portrayed as the ideal image of humanity. *David* by Michelangelo Buonarroti (1475–1564).

> *The extraordinary expression, 'making love', 'to make love', might have lent sexuality, the joining of men and women in wholeness, a very special place in Christian thought, instead of which we have scorned and denied the marvellous gift.*
>
> MONICA FURLONG,
> ENGLISH WRITER

are used in justification – such as Leviticus 18:22 and 20:13 and Romans 1:27, in which sex between two males is specifically referred to as an abomination. In recent years, this teaching has been challenged by gay and lesbian groups who want their voices to be heard and their way of life accepted. They argue that

the gospel of Christ is above all about love and acceptance, freedom and justice, and that to exclude people from the Church is wrong. The response of Christians has varied, from the liberal inclusive approach at one extreme, to the conservative upholding of traditional teaching at the other, with many shades of opinion in between. The specific issue of whether practising homosexuals can become priests or ministers is causing division in many mainstream denominations.

THE LAMBETH CONFERENCE, 1998

Every 10 years the bishops of the world's 55 million Anglicans gather together for the Lambeth Conference. In 1998 the debate over the place of sexually active homosexuals overshadowed much of the three-week conference. The bishops voted 526 to 70 with 45 abstentions for a resolution declaring that homosexual practice is 'incompatible with scripture'. Other major Protestant Church bodies have also issued statements either rejecting ordination and marriage for practising homosexuals or affirming that sexual relations should be limited to heterosexual marriage. The vote at the Lambeth Conference signalled the increasing influence of African and Asian bishops. Bishop John Rucyahana of Shyira, Rwanda, is one example of a new generation of Church leaders from the developing countries who have been tested by internal warfare, religious persecution and poverty. 'The Church', he said, 'is losing the ability to preach the gospel of our Lord Jesus Christ. We don't like your First World way of speaking ambiguous words and not being straight on the issues.'

New Communities

One of the striking features of contemporary Christianity is the growth of new Christian communities. These are largely formed by laypeople and not part of any traditional religious order. They are expressions of diversification and renewal.

The new communities tend to be radical in their aims and usually offer an alternative lifestyle to members.

Taizé

Founded during the Second World War by Roger Schütz and Max Thurien in Burgundy in France, Taizé is an ecumenical, semi-monastic community with members from both Protestant and Catholic Churches. It is especially popular with young people and large numbers come from all over the world to stay for a week or more and share in the life of the community. Increasing numbers come from Eastern Europe. Taizé holds an annual meeting of around 100,000 young people in various European cities, and

The distinctive music of Taizé is used by Churches and Christian groups worldwide. Worship in the Church of the Reconciliation at Taizé, France.

> *The making of community is essentially a revolutionary act. It proposes to detach men and women from their dependence upon the dominant institutions of the world system and creates an alternative corporate reality based upon different social values.*
>
> JIM WALLIS, NORTH AMERICAN CHRISTIAN ACTIVIST, WRITER AND FOUNDER OF THE SOJOURNERS COMMUNITY

The monastic centre on the island of Iona was created by an Irish prince, Columba. From Iona the gospel spread throughout Scotland, and in the following generation, influenced much of northern England.

many of the community's monks live in slums throughout the world. Perhaps the most well-known aspect of Taizé is its music which is predominantly simple, short, repetitive chanting, often in Latin, and can be sung by people of all nationalities.

The Brüderhof
The Brüderhof were formed in 1920 by a group of Germans under the leadership of Eberhard Arnold (1883–1935). The new community had to leave Germany during the Second World War, and resettled in Paraguay, before finally moving to New York State. The Brüderhof support themselves by making toys and by printing books. They are pacifists and conservative on many theological matters such as the role of women. At the end of the 20th century the community joined with the Hutterites. It has become one

of the longest-enduring non-monastic communities.

Iona
Iona is a small island off the west coast of Scotland. It was made into a mission station by the Celtic saint, Columba, in 565 CE, and some believe that one of the world's most beautiful manuscripts, the *Book of Kells*, was created there. Today Iona is famous for its ecumenical community founded by George MacLeod in the 1930s, which teaches Christian spirituality, including prayer, meditation and social action. Pilgrims flock to Iona for retreats in the restored abbey, surrounded by ancient Celtic crosses.

Christianity and Other Faiths

With the growth of the 'global village', the world's religions have become less distant from each other. This had led to a challenge for Christians: should they remain aloof and only engage with people of different faiths in an attempt to evangelize them or should they seek dialogue and understanding?

The Bible teaches that Jesus Christ is the way, the truth and the life, and that no one comes to God except through him. For Christians, therefore, Christ is unique and Christianity not just one religion among many, but *the* way to truth and freedom.

There is deep division among Christians about the best way to approach those of other faiths. For some, recognizing any non-Christian practice or religion as worthwhile is akin to denying the saving power of the Christian gospel. For others, Christianity has been too triumphalist and arrogant in its approach; they feel that the activity of God outside the Christian Church must be acknowledged. The debate is only likely to get fiercer as the other faiths, especially Islam, grow in influence.

Judaism

Those prepared to dialogue with other religions in an attempt to understand them have made significant strides in recent times. The Holocaust of the Second World War was in many ways a turning point. Many Christians were guilty either of ignoring the evidence for the mass genocide or of acting as dutiful administrators of the appalling events. Jewish-Christian dialogue has increased in recent years, and more and more Christians are becoming interested in the writings of Jewish figures such as Martin Buber (1878–1965) and Elie Wiesel (1928–).

Islam

Understanding and dialoguing with Islam have been more of a challenge for Christians because of the long history of hostility between the two religions and the perception that many Muslims are extreme fundamentalists. However, when Muslims and Christians do enter into dialogue they often discover common ground: they have similar criticisms of Western culture, both honour a holy book and they have similar founding fathers, including Abraham, the father of Judaism, Christianity and Islam.

Hinduism and Buddhism

The spirituality of Hinduism and Buddhism has impressed many in the Western world in recent times. Christian yoga and Christian Zen are practised by increasing numbers of people in the West; leaders in this development include Bede Griffiths (1906–93) and Thomas Merton (1915–1968). Among Buddhists who are highly regarded by many Christians are the Dalai Lama (1935–) from Tibet and Thich Nhat Hanh (1926–) from Vietnam.

> *Let us be clear, then, that it is not our business to protect the truth. Rather it is our business to serve the truth, wherever and whenever it is found.*
>
> CHOAN-SENG SONG,
> TAIWANESE THEOLOGIAN

Thomas Merton with the Dalai Lama at Dharamsala, India. Merton was a Catholic monk who studied Eastern religions and identified with their rejection of many of the values of Western society.

Rapid Factfinder

A

absolution: forgiveness and release from guilt of a person following confession of their sin to a priest.

Advent: start of the Christian year; four weeks before Christmas; time of preparation for Christmas.

altar: table on which the sacrifice of the Mass is celebrated; originally wooden but later stone; retained by the Catholic and Anglican Churches after the Reformation; replaced in Reformed Churches by the Communion table.

Anglican: coined in the 19th century to describe Christians worldwide who are in communion with the diocese of Canterbury.

Apocrypha: section in Protestant Bibles separate from the Old and New Testaments containing a number of later Jewish works, written in Greek rather than in Hebrew; 'deuterocanonical' books of secondary importance included in the Roman Catholic Old Testament.

apostle: 'to send'; title for the disciples sent out by Jesus to spread the gospel.

Apostles' Creed: statement of faith first used about 390 CE; probably initially a baptismal confession; used in the Anglican Church.

Ascension Day: day on which some Christians remember the ascension of Jesus into heaven at the end of his life; known by Catholics as the Day of Obligation.

Ash Wednesday: first day of Lent; named after the Catholic practice of smearing the burnt ashes of palms from the previous Palm Sunday on the foreheads of worshippers.

atonement: 'at-one-ment', 'reconciliation', 'making amends'; reconciliation between God and human beings through the death and resurrection of Jesus.

Ave Maria: 'hail Mary'; first two words of the Latin prayer to the Virgin Mary used in Roman Catholic services.

B

baptism: rite of initiation into the Christian faith in many Churches; either baptism of infants (in Catholic, Orthodox and some Protestant Churches) or of believing adults (in the Baptist Church).

baptism in the Holy Spirit: outpouring of the Holy Spirit upon believers common in Pentecostal and charismatic Churches; may result in spiritual gifts such as the speaking of tongues or prophecy.

Baptist Church: major Protestant denomination formed in the 17th century; practises believer's baptism by immersion as a condition of Church membership.

believer's baptism: baptism of believing adults in the Baptist Church and other Reformed Churches.

Bible: collection of scriptural writings sacred to Jewish and Christian communities.

bishop: highest of the three major orders in the Christian Church, the other two being priest and deacon; in the Catholic Church the bishops are the successors of the apostles.

Bishop of Rome: formal title given to the Pope; St Peter is believed to have been the first holder of the position.

Breaking of Bread: a favourite term in many Reformed Churches for the service of Communion; taken from Acts 2:42.

C

Candlemas: 2 February; day on which all the candles needed for the coming year are consecrated in the Catholic Church.

canon: list of books recognized as authoritative by the Christian Church; the Church accepted the Jewish canon of 39 books plus the 27 books of the New Testament.

cathedral: church containing the throne (*cathedra*) of the bishop of the diocese; the mother church of the diocese.

Catholic Church: see Roman Catholic Church.

Catholic Patriotic Association: one of two state Churches set up by the Chinese government and under its control.

charismatic church: church of any denomination which recognizes the gifts of the Holy Spirit and uses them in its worship.

chrism: consecrated oil used in the Roman Catholic and Orthodox Churches in baptism, confirmation, ordination and anointing-the-sick services.

chrismation: anointing of a newly baptized child by the bishop or priest in the Eastern Orthodox Church; equivalent to confirmation in other Churches.

Christmas: festival celebrated worldwide to commemorate the birth of Jesus.

Church of England: Church in England which severed its connection with Rome under Henry VIII and subsequently under Elizabeth I in the 16th century; its doctrinal changes are embodied in the revised version of the Book of Common Prayer from 1552.

citadel: building in which members of the Salvation Army gather for their worship; place of refuge and security.

Communion: Eucharist; central sacrament of most Christian Churches.

confirmation: rite of admission into full membership of the Church; usually involves the laying on of hands by a bishop.

convent: buildings inhabited by a female religious community.

Coptic Church: the native Christian Church in Egypt, believed to have been founded by St Mark.

creation-centred spirituality: belief adhered to by Matthew Fox, among others, that celebrates the feminine side of God and the blessedness of the human body.

Creed: formal statement of Christian belief; the earliest Creeds were short baptismal formulae; the Apostles' and Nicene Creeds play important roles in some Christian worship.

crucifix: image of Jesus on the cross; seen in all Catholic and some Lutheran church buildings.

D

Day of Pentecost: Jewish festival held 50 days after Passover; day on which the Holy Spirit descended on the apostles after the ascension of Jesus; birthday of the Christian Church.

deacon: 'servant'; lowest order in Christian ministry below bishop and priest; now the preliminary step to becoming a priest; layperson involved in running the church in Presbyterian and Reformed Churches.

diocese: area under the authority of a bishop.

E

Easter: Christian Church's most joyful festival; celebration of Jesus' resurrection from the dead.

Easter Sunday: day on which Jesus rose from the dead; celebrated annually by Christians.

Eastern Orthodox Church: section of the Christian Church dominant in the East; formed after the split with the Western Catholic Church in 1054; its worship is based upon seven sacraments.

ecumenical movement: movement born in Edinburgh in 1910 that has sought to increase cooperation between different Christian Churches.

Enlightenment: term used to describe progress made in scientific, humanitarian, rationalist and liberal Western thought in the 18th century; also known as the Age of Reason

Epiphany: 'revelation'; festival held on 6 January to commemorate the manifestation of Christ to the Gentiles.

Episcopal Church: the Anglican Church in Scotland and the USA.

epistles: 'letters'; letters contained in the New Testament, written by Paul, Peter, John and other early Church leaders to instruct young churches in the Christian faith.

Essenes: Jewish fraternity, originating in the second century BCE, who lived a monastic life in the desert areas of Palestine.

Eucharist: 'thanksgiving'; one of several terms used for the sacrament of Communion.

evangelism: work of spreading the gospel considered to be the responsibility of all Christians.

Extreme Unction: one of the seven sacraments of the Roman Catholic and Eastern Orthodox Churches; the anointing with oil of a dying person; now usually called the anointing of the sick.

F

font: receptacle for water that occupies a permanent place in many churches; holds the water to be used in infant baptism.

G

Gentile: one who is not a Jew; term especially applied to Christians.

Good Friday: holy Friday; two days before Easter Day; commemorates the crucifixion of Jesus.

Gospels: 'good news'; first four books of the New Testament, ascribed to Matthew, Mark, Luke and John.

Great Fast: four weeks of fasting which precede the fast of Lent in the Eastern Orthodox Church.

Great Vigil: service in the Russian Orthodox Church to welcome Easter morning which starts at midnight and goes on till dawn.

Gregorian plainsong: unaccompanied singing of liturgical texts whose rhythm follows the accent of the words.

H

Hail Mary: first two words of the Latin prayer to the Virgin Mary used in Roman Catholic services; also called the Ave Maria.

high altar: main altar in a church; particularly used for the altar in an Eastern Orthodox church building.

Holy Liturgy: service incorporating the sacrament of Communion in the Eastern Orthodox Church; also called the Divine Liturgy.

holy orders: three orders of hierarchy or ranks in the Church: priest, bishop and deacon; one of seven sacraments in the Roman Catholic and Orthodox Churches.

Holy Spirit: also known as the Holy Ghost; the third person of the Holy Trinity, often portrayed as a dove; believed to be the inspiration behind the holy scriptures.

Holy Week: last week of Lent, beginning on Palm Sunday, running through Maundy Thursday and Good Friday, and ending on Holy Saturday.

homily: a sermon in a Catholic Church.

I

icon: a painting or mosaic of Jesus Christ, the holy family or one of the saints; used in the Eastern Orthodox Church as an aid to devotion in church and in the home.

iconostasis: screen in Eastern Orthodox church buildings which separates the high altar from the congregation; covered with icons; the royal doors in the middle are flanked by figures of Christ and the Virgin Mary.

incarnation: 'to be made flesh'; belief that the Son of God took on human flesh and that Jesus is truly God and truly man.

indulgences: acts of merit performed to shorten temporal punishment in purgatory; doctrine held by the Roman Catholic Church.

infant baptism: sacrament of initiation into the Church by baptism of babies and children whose promises are renewed later at confirmation.

Iona community: ecumenical Christian community founded by George MacLeod in the 1930s on the island of Iona.

J

Jerusalem: city captured and extended by King David; home to Solomon's Temple; city in which Jesus was crucified; city sacred to Jews and Muslims.

Jesus Prayer: prayer widely used in the Eastern Orthodox Church, dating back to the sixth century.

John the Baptist: son of Elizabeth and Zechariah and cousin of Jesus; his preaching heralded the coming of Jesus the Messiah; baptized Jesus in the River Jordan.

K

kingdom of God: ushered in by Jesus; subject of most of Jesus' parables; Jesus taught it is still to come in its fullness.

L

Last Supper: last meal that Jesus ate with his disciples before he was arrested; provided the pattern for Communion.

lectern: stand at the front of a church that holds a Bible.

Lent: period of 40 days beginning on Ash Wednesday and leading up to Easter; observed by many Christians as a season of repentance and fasting.

Liturgy of the Faithful: second part of the Orthodox Holy Liturgy during which Communion takes place.

Liturgy of the Mass: second part of the Catholic Mass during which the congregation partakes in Communion.

Liturgy of the Word: first part of the Catholic Mass including the eading of three Bible passages nd the homily.

.ord's Prayer: prayer that Jesus aught his disciples as a model or all believers; the only universal Christian prayer; nown as the 'Our Father' y Catholics.

.ord's Supper: used by Paul when eferring to the service including he sacrament of Communion; lso known as the Eucharist, Mass nd Holy Liturgy; used by some Reformed Churches to refer to Communion.

M

Mass: 'dismissal'; Roman Catholic term for the service of Communion.

Maundy Thursday: day before Good Friday; associated with esus washing the feet of his lisciples and with the institution of Communion.

Messiah: 'anointed one'; figure xpected by the Jews for centuries s one who would liberate them rom their enemies; believed to be esus by Christians.

minister: leader of a Reformed Church who serves the ongregation.

monastery: a house, or group of buildings, in which a male eligious community lives.

N

Nestorian Church: heretical Church of the fifth century CE based on the teachings of Nestorius, patriarch of Constantinople.

New Testament: second group of holy books in the Bible that emanated from the emerging Christian Church during the first century.

Nicene Creed: short statement of belief first used in the late fifth century; used in the Eucharist of Roman Catholic, Anglican and Eastern Orthodox Churches.

nuptial Mass: special form of the Mass celebrated as part of the wedding service.

O

Old Testament: Christian term for the Jewish canonical books contained in the first part of the Christian Bible.

ordination: ritual by which a layperson is admitted to the ministry of the Roman Catholic, Orthodox and Anglican Churches.

original sin: doctrine that there is a link between the sin of the first man and woman and the sin of all humankind ever since.

Our Father: used by Catholics to refer to the Lord's Prayer.

P

Palm Sunday: day at the start of Holy Week when Christians celebrate the entry of Jesus into Jerusalem on a donkey.

parish: area under the spiritual care of an Anglican or Roman Catholic priest.

paschal candle: tall candle lit in church services for the 40 days between Easter Day and Ascension Day.

Passover: annual Jewish festival celebrating the release of the Jewish people from Egyptian slavery under the leadership of Moses; festival during which Jesus was crucified.

Paul: outstanding leader of the early Church; undertook three missionary journeys; founded many churches around the Mediterranean; writer of many New Testament epistles.

penance: penalty placed on a person by the priest during confession for them to show true contrition for their sins.

penitent: person making the confession to a priest.

Pentecost: Jewish harvest festival which also celebrated the giving of the Torah to Moses on Mount Sinai; also called Shavuot and the Festival of Weeks.

Pentecostal Church: Reformed Church formed at the beginning of the 20th century whose worship is based upon the exercising of the gifts of the Holy Spirit.

Peter: most dominant of the 12 disciples; first leader of the early Church; believed by Catholics to have been the first Pope and Bishop of Rome.

Pharisees: major Jewish sect at the time of Jesus; mentioned in the Gospels as frequently leading the opposition to Jesus.

Plymouth Brethren: sect of evangelical Christians founded in Ireland in 1828; still found in England and USA.

Pontius Pilate: Roman procurator of Judea between 26 and 36 CE; responsible for ordering the execution of Jesus.

Pope: 'papa'; leader of the Roman Catholic Church; believed to be the successor to Peter as Bishop of Rome.

priest: official minister of religion in the Roman Catholic, Orthodox and some Protestant Churches; ordained and so qualified to dispense the sacraments.

prophecy: ability to speak insightful words of wisdom through the empowerment of the Holy Spirit; one of the spiritual gifts listed by Paul in 1 Corinthians 12.

prophet: man or woman sent by God to deliver a divine message.

Prophets: one of three sections in the Jewish scriptures, divided into Major Prophets (Isaiah, Jeremiah, Ezekiel and Daniel) and Minor Prophets (Hosea through to Malachi).

Protestant: member of a Church that is not Roman Catholic or Orthodox; Church based on the teachings of the Reformation.

pulpit: raised or enclosed platform at the front of a church; place from which the sermon is delivered.

purgatory: place where Roman Catholics believe almost everyone spends time after death; intermediate place between heaven and hell; place of purification and preparation for heaven.

Q

Quakers: Reformed denomination founded in the 17th century; based on the teachings of George Fox; emphasize silence in worship and nonviolence; also known as the Society of Friends.

R

rabbi: Jewish teacher.

reconciliation: sacrament of the Roman Catholic Church; involves the confession of sins to a priest and the granting of absolution.

Reformation: religious revolution in the 16th century; led to the break-up of the Catholic Church and the formation of many Reformed Churches.

Reformed Churches: Churches, such as Lutheran, Anglican, Baptist and Methodist, that follow the teachings of the Reformation, especially the supremacy of the Bible in all Church life.

relic: physical remains of a saint or holy person to which worship or veneration is given; sanctioned in the Roman Catholic Church, but not in Protestant Churches.

Requiem Mass: form of Mass used in the Roman Catholic Church during a funeral.

reserved sacrament: consecrated bread and wine kept in the tabernacle in a Roman Catholic church and used for Communion.

resurrection: rising of Jesus from from the dead three days after being crucified; central Christian belief.

Roman Catholic Church: community of believers throughout the world who accept the leadership of the Pope.

rosary: 'rose garden'; string of beads used by some Roman Catholics to help them to pray.

royal doors: doors in the middle of the iconostasis in an Orthodox church building through which

the priest walks when taking bread and wine from the high altar to the people during Holy Liturgy.

S

Sabbath: 'to rest'; seventh day of the week kept by Jews as a day for rest and relaxation.

sacrament: outward, visible sign of an inward, spiritual blessing obtained through a rite of the Christian Church.

Sadducees: influential priestly Jewish group at the time of Jesus; the High Priest was always a Sadducee.

saint: person recognized for the holiness of their life; the Roman Catholic Church canonizes such people after their death.

Salvation Army: Protestant organization formed in the middle of the 19th century; well known for its work among the poor and underprivileged.

Sanhedrin: highest Jewish tribunal at the time of Jesus; had 71 members and met in Jerusalem; condemned Jesus to death before he was taken in front of Pontius Pilate.

Satan: 'adversary' or 'enemy'; name traditionally applied to the Devil; the personification of evil.

Second Coming: belief that Jesus will return to the earth in the future to set up God's kingdom.

Second Vatican Council: council of the Roman Catholic Church held between 1962 and 1965, made many decisions which modernized the worship of the Catholic Church.

havuot: Jewish Feast of Weeks - Pentecost; commemorated the giving of the law to Moses on Mount Sinai.

bema: 'hear'; Jewish name for the words of Deuteronomy 6:4; basic statement of Jewish belief in the oneness of God.

Shrove Tuesday: day before Ash Wednesday; day before Lent begins; day of feasting before the fasting of Lent.

sign of the cross: rite carried out by Orthodox and Catholic Christians; involves 'drawing' the shape of the cross over their bodies using holy water.

speaking in tongues: ability to speak in a foreign or unfamiliar language through the empowerment of the Holy Spirit; one of the spiritual gifts listed by Paul in 1 Corinthians 12.

stations of the cross: pictures or sculptures around the outside wall of a Roman Catholic church indicating 14 places where Jesus is thought to have stopped on the way to crucifixion.

stoup: container just inside the door of a Roman Catholic church; contains the holy water that people use to make the sign of the cross.

Sunday: day adopted by Christians for worship; first day of the week.

synagogue: 'coming together'; Jewish meeting place for prayer and instruction in the scriptures; place which houses the scrolls of the Law (the Torah).

Synoptic Gospels: three Gospels (Matthew, Mark and Luke) that take a similar approach to the life of Jesus and have much material in common.

T

tabernacle: receptacle in Roman Catholic churches for vessels containing the reserved sacrament; usually placed on, above or to one side of the altar.

Taizé chant: simple, short, repetitive phrases sung in Latin; developed by the Taizé community.

Taizé community: semi-monastic order whose members are from both Roman Catholic and Protestant traditions; founded at Taizé in France during the Second World War by Roger Schutz and Max Thurien.

Temple: first built in Jerusalem around 950 BCE by Solomon; destroyed by the Babylonians in 586 BCE; rebuilt by Herod the Great beginning in 19 BCE, finally destroyed by the Romans in 70 CE.

Ten Commandments: part of the Torah; 10 laws given by God to Moses on Mount Sinai; foundation of Jewish and Christian moral and spiritual living.

Three-Self Patriotic Movement: one of two state Churches in China set up by and under the watchful eye of the government; based on the ideals of self-support, self-government and self-propagation.

Torah: first five books of the Jewish scriptures; books of the Law; considered to be God's greatest gift to the Jewish people.

transubstantiation: Roman Catholic belief that the bread and the wine in the Mass become the actual body and blood of Jesus during the prayer of consecration.

Trinity: Christian belief in one God in three persons: Father, Son and Holy Spirit.

U

United Church: Congregationalists merged with evangelical and Reformed Churches.

V

virgin birth: belief held by many Christians that Mary was a virgin when she conceived Jesus, the father being the Holy Spirit; the Roman Catholic Church holds that Mary remained a virgin for the whole of her life.

Virgin Mary: Mary, the Mother of Jesus; the focus of much devotion in the Roman Catholic Church.

votive candles: small candles lit by Catholic worshippers before offering a prayer in church.

W

Whitsun: 'white Sunday'; also known as Pentecost; festival at which Christians remember the giving of the Holy Spirit to the first Christians.

Z

Zealots: fanatical group at the time of Jesus; dedicated to forcibly removing the Roman army from Palestine.

Picture Acknowledgments

Abbey of Gethsemani: p. 153. Used by permission of the Abbey of Gethsemani, Kentucky, USA.

David Alexander: p. 33.

Andes Press Agency: pp. 134–35 (© Carlos Reyes-Manzo), 150 (© Alain Pinoges).

The Art Archive: pp. 8 (*The Crucifixion* [fresco] by the School of Giotto: San Francesco, Assisi/Dagli Orti), 32 (*Moses Receives Tablets of the Ten Commandments on Mount Sinai* [fresco, 16th century]: Sucevita Monastery, Moldova, Romania/Dagli Orti), 50 (*The Baptism of Christ* [cupola mosaic, before 526]: Baptistery of Arians/Dagli Orti), 62 (Biblioteca Nazionale Palermo/Dagli Orti), 62–63 (Dagli Orti), 70 (*Portrait of Henry VIII* by Hans Holbein the Younger [1497/9–1543]: Windsor Castle).

Art Directors & TRIP Photo Library: pp. 7 (D. Butcher), 105 (K. Cardwell), 116 (D. Butcher), 117 (bottom, D. Butcher), 119 (bottom, D. Butcher), 131 (Billy Graham preaching at a rally in Anaheim, California: S. Grant), 132–33 (D. Butcher), 134 (top, D. Butcher).

Baptist Missionary Society: p. 77 (bottom).

Board of Trinity College, Dublin: p. 30 (ms. 58, fol. 34r).

Bodleian Library, University of Oxford: pp. 23 (Corpus Christi College, ms. 410, fol. 169v), 28 (ms. douce 144, fol. 131), 36 (ms. Auct. T. inf. I.10, fol. 17v–22), 58 (ms. Rawl. Liturg. f.26, fol. 7r–169v, fol. 117), 96 (ms. Hatton 48, fol. 24v–25), 106 (Keble College, ms. 49, fol. 167v).

Bridgeman Art Library: pp. 2 (middle, *Martin Luther* [panel] by Lucas Cranach the Elder [1472–1553]: Kurpfalzisches Museum, Heidelberg, Germany/Giraudon), 16 (*Christ Washing the Disciples' Feet* [c. 1390] by the Italian School [14th century], Arezzo: Christie's Images, London, UK), 68 (*Martin Luther* [panel] by Lucas Cranach the Elder [1472–1553]: Kurpfalzisches Museum, Heidelberg, Germany/Giraudon), 69 (*Portrait of John Calvin* [French theologian and reformer, 1509–64] [oil on canvas] by the Swiss School [17th century]: collection of Albert Rilliet, Geneva, Switzerland/Giraudon/Lauros), 76 (*Crusaders Bombard Nicea with Heads* [c. 1098] from *Estoire d'Outremer* [12th century] by William of Tyre [c. 1130–85]: Bibliothèque National, Paris, France, Fr. 2630, fol. 22v), 77 (top, *Saint Ignatius of Loyola* [1491–1556] [oil on canvas] by the French School [17th century]: Chateau de Versailles, France/Giraudon/Lauros), 90–91 (*Jesus Washing Peter's Feet* [1876] by Ford Madox Brown [1821–93]: Manchester City Art Galleries, UK), 144 (*St Francis Preaching to the Birds* [1296–97] by Giotto di Bondone [c. 1266–1337]: San Francesco, Upper Church, Assisi, Italy), 148 (*David* [marble, 1501–1504] by Michelangelo Buonarroti [1475–1564]: Galleria dell'Accademia, Florence, Italy).

The British Library: pp. 15 (scenes from the *Octateuch*, Or. 481, fol. 156v), 101 (from *The Travels of Sir John Mandeville* [15th century], Add. 24189, fol. 9 [WF]). By permission of The British Library.

The British Museum: p. 39.

Susanna Burton: pp. 3 (middle), 5, 81, 82 (both), 83, 87, 95, 118, 139 (bottom).

Faith Cummins: p. 138.

Flower Pentecostal Heritage Center, Springfield, MO, USA: p. 132.

Hutchison Picture Library: pp. 42–43 (© V. Birgus), 56 (© John G. Egan), 78–79 (© Bernard Regent), 80–81 (© Eric Lawrie), 84 (© Maurice Harvey), 85 (© Michael MacIntyre), 97 (top, © Nigel Howard), 100 (© Anna Tully), 108–109 (© Edward Parker), 110–11 (© John Hatt), 121 (© Ingrid Hudson), 123 (© Angela Silvertop), 124 (© Jeremy Horner), 125 (© Andrey Zvoznikov), 137 (top, Pope John Paul II, 1982, Benin, © Anna Tully).

John Williams Studios: p. 120.

Jon Arnold Images: pp. 28–29.

Alex Keene (The Walking Camera): pp. 4–5, 12, 19, 35, 40, 41, 55, 64, 65, 67, 73, 94, 97, 103, 112, 113, 114, 115, 117 (top), 119 (top), 122.

Roger Kent: p. 44 (© Roger Kent).

Lion Publishing: pp. 2–3 (David Beaton), 13 (David Townsend), 21 (David Townsend), 74–75, 102 (© Benedettine di Priscilla), 104–105, 108, 109, 130, 140, 15

Magnum Photos Ltd: p. 141 (© Bob Adelman).

Museo Nacional del Prado, Madrid: pp. 48–49 (*The Bound Lamb* [*Agnus Dei*] by Francisco de Zurbaran [1598–1664])

The National Gallery, London: pp. 3 (*Imago Pietatis*, Italian, Venetian [14th century]), 20–21 (*The Betrayal of Christ* by Ugolino di Nerio [active 1317, died c. 1339/49]), 25 (*Pentecost* by Giotto di Bondone [c. 1267–1337]), 26 (*St Pete* by the Master of the Palazzo Venezia Madonna [active mid-14th century]), 45 (*The Trinity* by Jacopo di Cione [active c. 1362, died 1398/1400]), 47 (*The Adoration of the Shepherds* by Rembrandt van Rijn [1606–69]), 53 (*Imago Pietatis*, Italian, Venetian [14th century]), 93 (*The Woman Taken in Adultery* by Rembrandt van Rijn [1606–69]), 99 (*Adoring Saints* by Jacopo di Cione [active c. 1362, died 1398/1400]), 127 (*Pentecost* by Barnaba da Modena [active 1361–83]).

National Portrait Gallery, London: p. 73 (top, *Portrait of John Wesley* [1766] by Nathaniel Hone [1718–84]). By courtesy of the National Portrait Gallery, London.

Open Doors International & Gospel Films, Inc: p. 143.

Oxford Scientific Films: p. 145 (© Alan and Sandy Carey).

John Rogers (Frank Spooner Pictures Ltd): pp. 72, 114–15.

Nicholas Rous: p. 139 (top).

Superstock: pp. 22 (*The Crucifixion* by Tintoretto [1518–94]: Christie's Images), 146 (*Madonna Litta* by Leonardo da Vinci [1452–1519]: Hermitage Museum, St Petersburg, Russia).

Graham Tomlin: p. 71. Used by permission of the Augustinian Monastery in Erfurt.

Derek West: front endpaper, p. 10.

World Council of Churches: pp. 2 (left, © Peter Williams/WCC), 6, 60–61 (© Peter Williams/WCC), 128–29 (Peter Williams), 136–37, 137 (© Peter Williams/WCC), 147 (© Peter Williams/WCC).

Andrew Whittuck: pp. 88–89.